Working Women

Other Books of Related Interest:

Opposing Viewpoints Series

Feminism

Gender Roles

Work and Family

At Issue Series

Are Women Paid Fairly?

Current Controversies Series

The Wage Gap

Women in Politics

"Congress shall make no law ... abridging the freedom of speech, or of the press."

First Amendment to the US Constitution

The basic foundation of our democracy is the First Amendment guarantee of freedom of expression. The Opposing Viewpoints series is dedicated to the concept of this basic freedom and the idea that it is more important to practice it than to enshrine it.

Working Women

Noah Berlatsky, Book Editor

GREENHAVEN PRESS
A part of Gale, Cengage Learning

GALE
CENGAGE Learning·

Farmington Hills, Mich • San Francisco • New York • Waterville, Maine
Meriden, Conn • Mason, Ohio • Chicago

Patricia Coryell, *Vice President & Publisher, New Products & GVRL*
Douglas Dentino, *Manager, New Products*
Judy Galens, *Acquisitions Editor*

For more information, contact:
Greenhaven Press
27500 Drake Rd.
Farmington Hills, MI 48331-3535
Or you can visit our Internet site at gale.cengage.com

For product information and technology assistance, contact us at

Gale Customer Support, 1-800-877-4253
For permission to use material from this text or product, submit all requests online at
www.cengage.com/permissions

Further permissions questions can be emailed to permissionrequest@cengage.com

Articles in Greenhaven Press anthologies are often edited for length to meet page requirements. In addition, original titles of these works are changed to clearly present the main thesis and to explicitly indicate the author's opinion. Every effort is made to ensure that Greenhaven Press accurately reflects the original intent of the authors. Every effort has been made to trace the owners of copyrighted material.

Cover Image copyright © auremar/Shutterstock.com.

LIBRARY OF CONGRESS CATALOGING-IN-PUBLICATION DATA

Working women / Noah Berlatsky, book editor.
   pages cm. -- (Opposing viewpoints)
   Includes bibliographical references and index.
   ISBN 978-0-7377-7302-6 (hardcover) -- ISBN 978-0-7377-7303-3 (pbk.)
  1. Women--Employment--Juvenile literature. 2. Sex discrimination--Juvenile literature. 3. Discrimination in employment--Juvenile literature. I. Berlatsky, Noah.
  HD6053.W6747 2015
  331.4--dc23

                            2014040159

Printed in Mexico
1 2 3 4 5 6 7 19 18 17 16 15

Contents

Why Consider Opposing Viewpoints?

> *"The only way in which a human being can make some approach to knowing the whole of a subject is by hearing what can be said about it by persons of every variety of opinion and studying all modes in which it can be looked at by every character of mind. No wise man ever acquired his wisdom in any mode but this."*
>
> *John Stuart Mill*

In our media-intensive culture it is not difficult to find differing opinions. Thousands of newspapers and magazines and dozens of radio and television talk shows resound with differing points of view. The difficulty lies in deciding which opinion to agree with and which "experts" seem the most credible. The more inundated we become with differing opinions and claims, the more essential it is to hone critical reading and thinking skills to evaluate these ideas. Opposing Viewpoints books address this problem directly by presenting stimulating debates that can be used to enhance and teach these skills. The varied opinions contained in each book examine many different aspects of a single issue. While examining these conveniently edited opposing views, readers can develop critical thinking skills such as the ability to compare and contrast authors' credibility, facts, argumentation styles, use of persuasive techniques, and other stylistic tools. In short, the Opposing Viewpoints Series is an ideal way to attain the higher-level thinking and reading skills so essential in a culture of diverse and contradictory opinions.

In addition to providing a tool for critical thinking, Opposing Viewpoints books challenge readers to question their own strongly held opinions and assumptions. Most people form their opinions on the basis of upbringing, peer pressure, and personal, cultural, or professional bias. By reading carefully balanced opposing views, readers must directly confront new ideas as well as the opinions of those with whom they disagree. This is not to argue simplistically that everyone who reads opposing views will—or should—change his or her opinion. Instead, the series enhances readers' understanding of their own views by encouraging confrontation with opposing ideas. Careful examination of others' views can lead to the readers' understanding of the logical inconsistencies in their own opinions, perspective on why they hold an opinion, and the consideration of the possibility that their opinion requires further evaluation.

Evaluating Other Opinions

To ensure that this type of examination occurs, Opposing Viewpoints books present all types of opinions. Prominent spokespeople on different sides of each issue as well as well-known professionals from many disciplines challenge the reader. An additional goal of the series is to provide a forum for other, less known, or even unpopular viewpoints. The opinion of an ordinary person who has had to make the decision to cut off life support from a terminally ill relative, for example, may be just as valuable and provide just as much insight as a medical ethicist's professional opinion. The editors have two additional purposes in including these less known views. One, the editors encourage readers to respect others' opinions—even when not enhanced by professional credibility. It is only by reading or listening to and objectively evaluating others' ideas that one can determine whether they are worthy of consideration. Two, the inclusion of such viewpoints encourages the important critical thinking skill of objectively evaluating an author's credentials and bias. This evaluation will illuminate an author's reasons for taking a particular stance on an issue and will aid in readers' evaluation of the author's ideas.

It is our hope that these books will give readers a deeper understanding of the issues debated and an appreciation of the complexity of even seemingly simple issues when good and honest people disagree. This awareness is particularly important in a democratic society such as ours in which people enter into public debate to determine the common good. Those with whom one disagrees should not be regarded as enemies but rather as people whose views deserve careful examination and may shed light on one's own.

Thomas Jefferson once said that "difference of opinion leads to inquiry, and inquiry to truth." Jefferson, a broadly educated man, argued that "if a nation expects to be ignorant and free . . . it expects what never was and never will be." As individuals and as a nation, it is imperative that we consider the opinions of others and examine them with skill and discernment. The Opposing Viewpoints series is intended to help readers achieve this goal.

David L. Bender and Bruno Leone,
Founders

Introduction

"Yes, of course I do porn for money. It's a job, not a summer retreat. Why else do we labor at things if not to see a profit?"

—Belle Knox,
*"I Don't Want Your Pity:
Sex Work and Labor Politics,"*
Huffington Post, *April 14, 2014*

W omen's work has long been controversial; in some contexts, it has even been treated as scandalous or shocking. To some degree, this has changed. However, to some degree, it is still the case—as is demonstrated by a major news story of 2014, when it was revealed that a Duke University freshman was working in pornography. The student, who goes by the name Belle Knox, was outed by classmate Thomas Bagley, who recognized her from one of her videos. The story of a college student who was working in pornography went on to become a major national news story.

Belle Knox herself wrote an essay about the controversy at the online magazine *xoJane,* in which she said that many people had questioned her decision to work in the sex industry. She then went on to explain her motivations for working in pornography.

> The answer is actually quite simple. I couldn't afford $60,000 in tuition, my family has undergone significant financial burden, and I saw a way to graduate from my dream school free of debt, doing something I absolutely love. Because to be clear: My experience in porn has been nothing but supportive, exciting, thrilling and empowering.

Knox acknowledges that many women do not have a positive experience working in the pornography industry, but she argues in the *xoJane* article that the way to reduce such negative experiences is to "remove the stigma attached to their profession and treat it as a legitimate career that needs regulation and oversight. We need to give a voice to the women that are exploited and abused in the industry. Shaming and hurling names at them, the usual treatment we give sex workers, is *not* the way to achieve this."

Knox herself faced much abuse and harassment following her outing. Tyler Kingkade, writing at the *Huffington Post*, reported that Knox has been targeted both on campus and online. Her real name, which she has tried to keep private, has been posted on the web, along with the names of family members, causing Knox to fear for her family's safety. She no longer feels comfortable going to parties at Duke, where "either drunk guys will yell at me . . . or I have a bunch of girls glaring at me," she told Kingkade. Other students have written a stream of rape threats and death threats to her on Facebook and Twitter. "It was just like every single day things would get worse," she said. "I was getting a bunch of students tweeting me mean things. There were stares and whispers in the dining hall. After I was outed, every single day waking up was like a nightmare."

Knox has also been criticized by some writers who object to her claim that she has found her work empowering and fulfilling. Jess Carbino writing at the *Huffington Post* argues that "the overwhelming majority of sex workers, however, are not students selling sex to make a large sum of cash. . . . Rather than exercising agency over their bodies through selling sex, most sex workers are also forced to engage in sexual acts." For Carbino, sex work is not really work for most people, but exploitation. Carbino also argues that pornography serves to "objectify women and perpetuate sexual inequality."

Despite the harassment and criticism, though, Knox said in an interview with the *Duke Chronicle* that she had chosen work in pornography rather than employment in waitressing because "I worked as a waitress . . . for a year in high school and not only did it interfere with my school where I was barely sleeping and wasn't doing my work, but also I was making $400 a month after taxes. I felt like I was being degraded and treated like s--t. My boss was horrible to me." For Knox, she felt "more degraded" working in a blue-collar job for low pay than working in the pornography industry, where her salary was much higher and she felt she was treated with more respect.

Knox's situation is unusual in certain ways, but it also resonates with, or is connected to, issues that face women who work more broadly. Those issues include, for example, the difficulty women can face in making a living wage. They also include the ways women can be shamed for working or succeeding, the problems working women can face with harassment, and the question of whether work empowers women or exploits them. *Opposing Viewpoints: Working Women* explores these topics and others in chapters titled "Do Women Experience Discrimination at Work?," "How Does Motherhood Affect Working Women?," "Does the Lean-In Movement Help Working Women?," and "How Does Workplace Harassment Affect Working Women?" The topics examine the barriers women continue to face at work and what can be done to eliminate inequalities in the workplace.

Do Women Experience Discrimination at Work?

Chapter Preface

The Federal Reserve System controls American monetary policy. The chairman of the Board of Governors of the Federal Reserve is therefore one of the most powerful economic figures in the world. A recent controversy surrounding the appointment of a new chairman of the board brought into sharp focus issues regarding discrimination against women in the workplace.

When Ben Bernanke's term as chairman of the Federal Reserve ended in 2014, President Barack Obama suggested his longtime economic advisor Lawrence "Larry" Summers as Bernanke's replacement.

The choice sparked an unexpected uproar centering on Janet Yellen. Yellen had served as vice chair of the Federal Reserve under Bernanke from 2010 to 2014. Many people considered her the natural choice to succeed Bernanke and become the first woman to head the Federal Reserve. Ezra Klein, writing in the *Washington Post* on July 19, 2013, noted that Yellen was a "clear front-runner" for Fed chair; but, he said, "she's by no means a sure thing." According to Klein, "One important reason she's not—and I don't know another way to say this—is sexism, as evidenced by the whispering campaign that's emerged against her." Klein went on to describe how those pushing for Summers had said that Yellen, "lacks 'toughness.' She's short on 'gravitas.' Too 'soft-spoken' or 'passive.'" Klein argued that these were sexist stereotypes, showing that "monetary economics remains a bit of a boys' club."

Noam Scheiber writing in the *New Republic* on August 1, 2013, expanded on Klein's point, arguing that

> Summers benefits less from overt discrimination than a kind of subtle, institutionalized bias. Under this scenario, no one

with influence over the decision need be personally hostile to women—and, for the record, I don't believe any of them are. They simply happen to favor candidates who belong to a small, insular group of people that they know well, and very few women happen to belong to that group. As a variety of commentators have pointed out, this is basically how gender discrimination works in this day and age.

The debate about Summers was made even more acrimonious because of comments he made while president of Harvard University, in which he suggested that women may have less innate aptitude for math and science than men. Dave Johnson in a July 25, 2013, article at the *Huffington Post* suggested that such incidents "alone should disqualify [Summers] from consideration." On the other hand, Katharine Cook, writing for the American Enterprise Institute on August 2, 2013, argued that Summers's comments were not sexist and that "the opinion that President Obama should neglect to consider Summers on the basis of these remarks relies on a preference for politesse over proficiency, adherence to a creed of political correctness over qualification."

Because of the controversy, Summers withdrew his name from the nomination. Yellen was eventually appointed and confirmed as Federal Reserve chair. Questions about how bias and discrimination affect women's opportunities at high-level jobs, however, remain.

The authors in the following chapter examine issues surrounding discrimination against women in the workplace, including the gender pay gap and ways in which women can be discriminated against because of their appearances.

> *"Even after accounting for key factors that affect earnings ... our model could not explain all of the difference in earnings between men and women."*

The Gender Pay Gap Is the Result of Discrimination

Bryce Covert

Bryce Covert is economic policy editor at the ThinkProgress *blog and a contributor to the* Nation. *In the following viewpoint, she argues that women continue to be paid less than men for the same work. She cites a number of studies that suggest that even when women work in the same jobs as men, they are paid less; similarly, when women ask for raises, they are less likely to receive them. Covert suggests that ending workplace restrictions on disclosing salaries to coworkers could help, and she also argues for passage of the Fair Pay Act.*

As you read, consider the following questions:

1. To what does Diana Furchtgott-Roth attribute the pay gap, and why does Covert disagree with her?

Reprinted with permission from the August 15, 2012, issue of The Nation. For subscription information, call 1-800-333-8536. Portions of each week's Nation magazine can be accessed at http://www.thenation.com.

2. Why does Covert reject the idea that women are paid less because they don't ask for wage increases?

3. What does Covert say that the Paycheck Fairness Act would do?

I would love to agree with Ramesh Ponnuru's latest Bloomberg column, in which he argues that the gender wage gap—in which women on average still make seventy-seven cents for every dollar a man makes—is not caused by discrimination. Ponnuru argues that, rather, it's caused by different choices women make in their career paths and family formations. Wouldn't it be great if the gap didn't exist because women are held back and given less, but because they simply want different things? And it's certainly true that the fact that women are congregated in a different set of jobs and often have to leave the workforce when they have children plays a role. But even this can't explain away the gap.

The Gap Remains

Ponnuru cites research by conservative economist Diana Furchtgott-Roth and a consulting company showing that the gap all but disappears when factors such as women's working fewer hours, going part time or taking breaks from their careers are taken into account. But the Government Accountability Office [GAO] has already examined this question. The GAO tried to figure out just how much of the gap could be explained by these sorts of factors. To do so, it first performed a quantitative analysis using data from the Panel Study of Income Dynamics, a nationally representative longitudinal data set. It also supplemented that work by interviewing experts, reviewing the literature and contacting employers.

What did the study find? It's true that a variety of factors come into play—among them work patterns, job tenure, industry, occupation, race and marital status. But when it stripped all of these out, it still found that women earned about 80 percent of what men did. "Even after accounting for key factors that affect earnings," the authors report, "our model could not explain all of the difference in earnings between men and women." While it couldn't definitively say what caused that 20 percent gap, plain old discrimination was one of the few possibilities it highlighted.

The idea that women are paid less because they choose certain industries or occupations also doesn't get us very far. Among the Bureau of Labor Statistics's [BLS's] list of nearly 600 occupations, women make less than men in all but seven of them. And even in those where women make more, the difference is often as slight as a couple of dollars a week. They even make less in each industry: Among the BLS's thirteen industry categories, women make less than men in every single one. What this means is that even in "women's fields," men are going to rake in more. In fact, men have been entering traditionally female-dominated sectors during the recovery period, and as the *New York Times* noted, they're meeting with great success—"men earn more than women even in female-dominated jobs." Women can enter engineering all they want, but their pay still won't catch up to men's.

What of the idea that women are paid less because they don't ask for more money? Ponnuru argues that "women are less likely than men to drive hard bargains in salary negotiations," which might explain some of the gap. But that idea is based more on stereotypes of women shying away from ambition than reality. Research firm Catalyst found that women do in fact ask for more money—they just aren't rewarded for it. It looked at the career paths of thousands of MBA [master of business administration] graduates, men and women, who were similarly ambitious about their career paths. It found that among those who moved on from their first job, "there was no significant difference in the proportion of women and men who asked for increased compensation or a higher position." But there was a big difference in how much they ended up making—the women had slower compensation growth, and the gap got wider and wider as their careers progressed.

Unequal Rewards

Another recent study focused on the manager side of the equation: Are they rewarding men and women who seek raises equally? Turns out the answer is no. When managers were told they had a limited pot of money to give out in raises to employees with the same skill and experience levels, managers gave men raises that were two and a half times larger than women's when they knew they'd have to negotiate. In short: Women ask, but they don't receive.

Ponnuru does acknowledge that women's personal choices may be constrained by social expectations and structures. Indeed, when talking about the fact that many women drop out of the workforce to care for children or end up cutting back their hours, we're not just talking about fully equal options. Many women don't have a lot of other financial options— single mothers whose child care costs outpace their wages, parents who can't afford the incredible cost of child care, the fact that we are one of the three nations of 178 that doesn't guarantee paid maternity leave (not to mention paternity leave). That's why his claim that "there's no reason to think that women will ever, on average, have the same preferences as men about combining employment and parenthood" is doubtful. We haven't given them the chance.

Changes Can Be Made

So does this mean, as he tries to claim, that we can't look to employers to fix the gender wage gap? Should we throw up our hands? It's true that this is a complex issue that can't be solved with one silver bullet. But there are things that need to change in the workplace. Salary secrecy is a big one. How are women going to fight discrimination if they're barred, as about half of all workers are, from talking with their cowork-

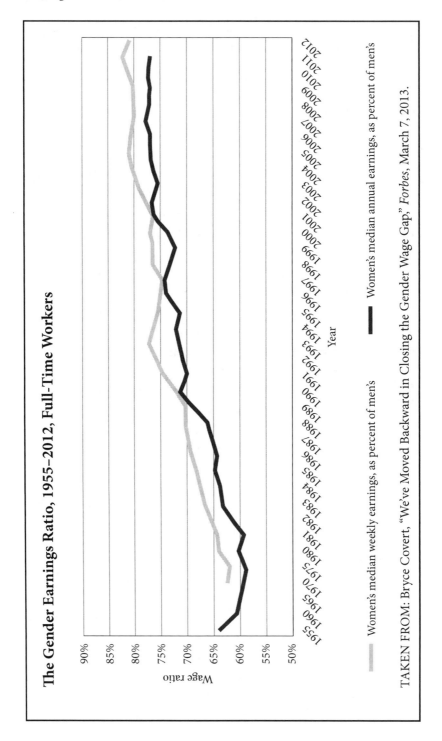

The Gender Earnings Ratio, 1955–2012, Full-Time Workers

Women's median weekly earnings, as percent of men's

Women's median annual earnings, as percent of men's

TAKEN FROM: Bryce Covert, "We've Moved Backward in Closing the Gender Wage Gap," *Forbes*, March 7, 2013.

ers about pay? Employers also have to fix a broken career pipeline that keeps equally ambitious women in lower pay jobs and prevents them from reaching the top ranks. Other solutions have to come from the government, such as guaranteeing paid family leave, increasing child care support so parents can afford quality choices and raising the minimum wage, since the vast majority of those workers are women.

Surely the gender wage gap is a complicated issue. But dismissing it as a figment of feminists' imagination, which seems to be a new conservative meme, is disingenuous. We can disagree on the solutions, but we shouldn't be fighting over the basic premise.

The Fair Pay Act

Update: Ramesh Ponnuru (very quickly!) responded to this piece, and I appreciate his civility. He doesn't dispute the findings of the GAO study I cite, but isn't convinced that the remaining 20 percent pay gap is due to discrimination. In some ways that's fair—the GAO is careful to say that it can't definitively pinpoint what's causing that remaining gap. It's incredibly hard to prove that it is in fact widespread discrimination. But I think some of the other points I made make a pretty good case that discrimination is going on. Take the study of managers: It was clear that they were biased against women, giving men raises that were more than double what they gave women. There have been other studies along these lines, like one that showed people identical résumés but with some mentioning that the applicant was a mother and others mentioning the applicant was a father. Fathers were offered $6,000 more than non-fathers in compensation; mothers were offered $11,000 less than non-mothers. Studies like these expose our deep-seated ideas about women in the workplace, held by men and women alike, that impact hiring and salary decisions.

He also points out that I didn't respond to the one piece of legislation he condemns in particular, which he calls the "comparable-worth bill called for by NOW." I'm not sure what bill he's referring to—in the press release he cites, NOW [National Organization for Women] mentions both the Paycheck Fairness Act (H.R. 1519/S. 797) and the Fair Pay Act (H.R. 1493). The Paycheck Fairness Act seeks to end pay secrecy—allowing employees to talk to one another about their compensation so that women can be made aware of any potential discrimination—and clarifies and strengthens the definition of what counts as a justification for pay disparities while beefing up the penalties for businesses that fail to provide equal compensation to proactively deter it.

Given Ponnuru's description, however, he likely means the Fair Pay Act. He claims that the bill would "force employers to change the pay scales for different jobs" and that "the government would be invited to decide appropriate pay levels, one lawsuit at a time." That's not quite what it does. It amends the Fair Labor Standards Act to prohibit discrimination in compensation on the basis of sex, race or national origin, while allowing exemptions for "seniority systems, merit systems, systems that measure earnings by quantity or quality of production, or differentials based on bona fide factors that the employer demonstrates are job-related or further legitimate business interests." It also prohibits firing or discriminating against employees for opposing anything the act makes illegal or assisting in an investigation, and it calls for the EEOC [Equal Employment Opportunity Commission] to study and report its effects. That doesn't sound like the government dictating wage scales—particularly given all of the exemptions for actual performance. If a company is paying a woman less than a man for any reason other than quality or quantity of work, seniority, merit or other defensible factors, what could possibly be the justification?

I'll reiterate that I don't think it will take one thing to close the wage gap—although, contra Ponnuru's statement, I do disagree with his assertion that "there's no reason to expect or want the gap ever to close completely." We can close the gap, but we have to address the many structural factors that go into it. These bills would take solid steps toward that goal, but they won't do it by themselves.

> *"Proofers often make the claim that women earn less than men doing the exact same job. They can't possibly know that."*

Why the Gender Gap Won't Go Away. Ever.

Kay S. Hymowitz

Kay S. Hymowitz is a contributing editor of City Journal, *the William E. Simon Fellow at the Manhattan Institute, and the author of* Manning Up: How the Rise of Women Has Turned Men into Boys. *In the following viewpoint, she argues that the pay gap is likely not caused by discrimination. Instead, she says, it is caused by women working fewer hours in less demanding jobs. She argues that women choose to do less work in order to spend more time with their children, and she concludes that policy changes and legislation will therefore not affect the gender pay gap.*

As you read, consider the following questions:

1. According to Hymowitz, what is the difference between hours worked by men working full time and women working full time?

Kay S. Hymowitz, "Why the Gender Gap Won't Go Away. Ever." *City Journal,* Summer 2011. © 2011 City Journal. Reproduced by permission.

2. Why does Hymowitz say that women work fewer hours and choose less demanding jobs than men?

3. What is the potential problem with the "mommy track," according to Hymowitz?

Early this past spring, the White House Council on Women and Girls released a much-anticipated report called "Women in America." One of its conclusions struck a familiar note: Today, as President Obama said in describing the document, "women still earn on average only about 75 cents for every dollar a man earns. That's a huge discrepancy."

It *is* a huge discrepancy. It's also an exquisite example of what journalist Charles Seife has dubbed "proofiness." Proofiness is the use of misleading statistics to confirm what you already believe. Indeed, the 75-cent meme depends on a panoply of apple-to-orange comparisons that support a variety of feminist policy initiatives, from the Paycheck Fairness Act to universal child care, while telling us next to nothing about the well-being of women.

This isn't to say that all is gender equal in the labor market. It is not. It also isn't to imply that discrimination against women doesn't exist or that employers shouldn't get more creative in adapting to the large number of mothers in the workplace. It does and they should. But by severely overstating and sensationalizing what is a universal predicament (I'm looking at you, Sweden and Iceland!), proofers encourage resentment-fueled demands that no government anywhere has ever fulfilled—and that no government ever will.

Let's begin by unpacking that 75-cent statistic, which actually varies from 75 to about 81, depending on the year and the study. The figure is based on the average earnings of full-time, year-round (FTYR) workers, usually defined as those who work 35 hours a week or more.

But consider the mischief contained in that "or more." It makes the full-time category embrace everyone from a clerk who arrives at her desk at 9 am and leaves promptly at 4 pm to a trial lawyer who eats dinner four nights a week—and lunch on weekends—at his desk. I assume, in this case, that the clerk is a woman and the lawyer a man for the simple reason that—and here is an average that proofers rarely mention—full-time men work more hours than full-time women do. In 2007, according to the Bureau of Labor Statistics, 27 percent of male full-time workers had workweeks of 41 or more hours, compared with 15 percent of female full-time workers; meanwhile, just 4 percent of full-time men worked 35 to 39 hours a week, while 12 percent of women did. Since FTYR men work more than FTYR women do, it shouldn't be surprising that the men, on average, earn more.

The way proofers finesse "full-time" can be a wonder to behold. Take a recent article in the *Washington Post* by Mariko Chang, author of a forthcoming book on the wealth gap between women and men. Chang cites a wage difference between "full-time" male and female pharmacists to show how "even when they work in the same occupation, men earn more." A moment's Googling led me to a 2001 study in the *Journal of the American Pharmacists Association* concluding that male pharmacists worked 44.1 hours a week, on average, while females worked 37.2 hours. That study is a bit dated, but it's a good guess that things haven't changed much in the last decade. According to a 2009 article in the *American Journal of Pharmaceutical Education*, female pharmacists' preference for reduced work hours is enough to lead to an industry labor shortage.

The other arena of mischief contained in the 75-cent statistic lies in the seemingly harmless term "occupation." Everyone knows that a CEO makes more than a secretary and that a computer scientist makes more than a nurse. And most people wouldn't be shocked to hear that secretaries and nurses are likely to be women, while CEOs and computer scientists are likely to be men. That obviously explains much of the wage gap.

But proofers often make the claim that women earn less than men *doing the exact same job*. They can't possibly know that. The Labor Department's occupational categories can be so large that a woman could drive a truck through them. Among "physicians and surgeons," for example, women make only 64.2 percent of what men make. Outrageous, right? Not if you consider that there are dozens of specialties in medicine: some, like cardiac surgery, require years of extra training, grueling hours, and life-and-death procedures; others, like pediatrics, are less demanding and consequently less highly rewarded. Only 16 percent of surgeons, but a full 50 percent of pediatricians, are women. So the statement that female doctors make only 64.2 percent of what men make is really on the order of a tautology, much like saying that a surgeon working 50 hours a week makes significantly more than a pediatrician working 37.

A good example of how proofers get away with using the rogue term "occupation" is "Behind the Pay Gap," a widely quoted 2007 study from the American Association of University Women whose executive summary informs us in its second paragraph that "one year out of college, women working full time earn only 80 percent as much as their male colleagues earn." The report divides the labor force into 11 extremely broad occupations determined by the Department of Education. So ten years after graduation, we learn, women who go into "business" earn considerably less than their male counterparts do. But the businessman could be an associate at Morgan Stanley who majored in econ, while the businesswoman could be a human-relations manager at Foot Locker who took a lot of psych courses. You don't read until the end of the summary—a point at which many readers will have already tweeted their indignation—that when you control for such factors as education and hours worked, there's actually just a 5 percent pay gap. But the AAUW isn't going to begin a report with the statement that women earn 95 percent of what their male counterparts earn, is it?

Now, while a 5 percent gap will never lead to a million-woman march on Washington, it's not peanuts. Over a year, it can add up to real money, and over decades in the labor force, it can mean the difference between retirement in a Boca Raton co-op and a studio apartment in the inner suburbs. Many studies have examined the subject, and a consensus has emerged that when you control for what researchers call "observable" differences—not just hours worked and occupation, but also marital and parental status, experience, college major, and industry—there is still a small unexplained wage gap between men and women. Two Cornell economists, Francine Blau and Lawrence Kahn, place the number at about 9 cents per dollar. In 2009, the CONSAD Research Corporation, under the auspices of the Labor Department, located the gap a little lower, at 4.8 to 7.1 percent.

So what do we make of what, for simplicity's sake, we'll call the 7 percent gap? You can't rule out discrimination, whether deliberate or unconscious. Many women say that male bosses are more comfortable dealing with male workers, especially when the job involves late-night meetings and business conferences in Hawaii. This should become a smaller problem over time, as younger men used to coed dorms and female roommates become managers and, of course, as women themselves move into higher management positions. It's also possible that male managers fear that a female candidate for promotion, however capable, will be more distracted by family matters than a male would be. They might assume that women are less able to handle competition and pressure. It's even possible that female managers think such things, too.

No, you can't rule out discrimination. Neither can you rule out other, equally plausible explanations for the 7 percent gap. The data available to researchers may not be precise; for instance, it's extremely difficult to find accurate measures of work experience. There's also a popular theory that women are less aggressive than men when it comes to negotiating salaries.

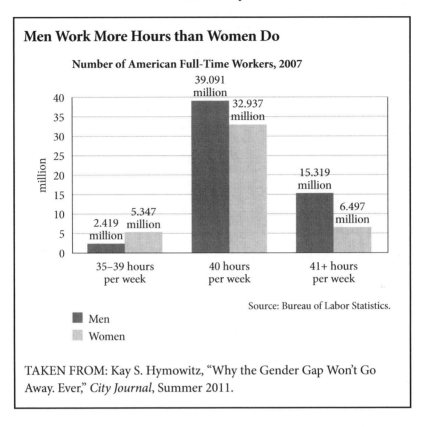

Men Work More Hours than Women Do

Number of American Full-Time Workers, 2007

Source: Bureau of Labor Statistics.

■ Men

▨ Women

TAKEN FROM: Kay S. Hymowitz, "Why the Gender Gap Won't Go Away. Ever," *City Journal*, Summer 2011.

The point is that we don't know the reason—or, more likely, reasons—for the 7 percent gap. What we do know is that making discrimination the default explanation for a wage gap, as proofers want us to do, leads us down some weird rabbit holes. Asian men and women earn more than white men and women do, says the Bureau of Labor Statistics. Does that mean that whites are discriminated against in favor of Asians? Female cafeteria attendants earn more than male ones do. Are men discriminated against in that field? Women who work in construction earn almost exactly what men in the field do, while women in education earn considerably less. The logic of default discrimination would lead us to conclude that construction workers are more open to having female colleagues than educators are. With all due respect to the construction workers, that seems unlikely.

So why do women work fewer hours, choose less demanding jobs, and then earn less than men do? The answer is obvious: kids. A number of researchers have found that if you consider only childless women, the wage gap disappears. June O'Neill, an economist who has probably studied wage gaps as much as anyone alive, has found that single, childless women make about 8 percent more than single, childless men do (though the advantage vanishes when you factor in education). Using Census Bureau data of pay levels in 147 of the nation's 150 largest cities, the research firm Reach Advisors recently showed that single, childless working women under 30 earned 8 percent more than their male counterparts did.

That's likely to change as soon as the children arrive. Mothers, particularly those with young children, take more time off from work; even when they are working, they're on the job less. "Behind the Pay Gap" found that "among women who graduated from college in 1992–93, more than one-fifth (23 percent) of mothers were out of the work force in 2003, and another 17 percent were working part time," compared with under 2 percent of fathers in each case. Other studies show consistently that the first child significantly reduces a woman's earnings and that the second child cuts them even further.

The most compelling research into the impact of children on women's careers and earnings—one that also casts light on why women are a rarity at the highest levels of the corporate and financial world—comes from a 2010 article in the *American Economic Journal* by Marianne Bertrand of the University of Chicago and Claudia Goldin and Lawrence Katz of Harvard. The authors selected nearly 2,500 MBAs who graduated between 1990 and 2006 from the University of Chicago's Booth School of Business and followed them as they made their way through the early stages of their careers. If there were discrimination to be found here, Goldin would be your woman. She is coauthor of a renowned 2000 study showing that blind auditions significantly increased the likelihood that an orchestra would hire female musicians.

Here's what the authors found: Right after graduation, men and women had nearly identical earnings and working hours. Over the next ten years, however, women fell way behind. Survey questions revealed three reasons for this. First and least important, men had taken more finance courses and received better grades in those courses, while women had taken more marketing classes. Second, women had more career interruptions. Third and most important, mothers worked fewer hours. "The careers of MBA mothers slow down substantially within a few years of first birth," the authors wrote. Though 90 percent of women were employed full time and year-round immediately following graduation, that was the case with only 80 percent five years out, 70 percent nine years out, and 62 percent ten or more years out—and only about half of women with children were working full time ten years after graduation. By contrast, almost all the male grads were working full time and year-round. Furthermore, MBA mothers, especially those with higher-earning spouses, "actively chose" family-friendly workplaces that would allow them to avoid long hours, even if it meant lowering their chances to climb the greasy pole.

In other words, these female MBAs bought tickets for what is commonly called the "mommy track." A little over 20 years ago, the *Harvard Business Review* published an article by Felice Schwartz proposing that businesses make room for the many, though not all, women who would want to trade some ambition and earnings for more flexibility and time with their children. Dismissed as the "mommy track," the idea was reviled by those who worried that it gave employers permission to discriminate and that it encouraged women to downsize their aspirations.

But as Virginia Postrel noted in a recent *Wall Street Journal* article, Schwartz had it right. When working mothers can, they tend to spend less time at work. That explains all those female pharmacists looking for reduced hours. It explains why female lawyers are twice as likely as men to go into public-interest law, in which hours are less brutal than in the partner track at Sullivan & Cromwell. Female medical students tell researchers that they're choosing not to become surgeons because of "lifestyle issues," which seems to be a euphemism for wanting more time with the kids. Thirty-three percent of female pediatricians are part-timers—and that's not because they want more time to play golf.

In the literature on the pay gap and in the media more generally, this state of affairs typically leads to cries of injustice. The presumption is that women pursue reduced or flexible hours because men refuse to take equal responsibility for the children and because the United States does not have "family-friendly policies." Child care is frequently described as a burden to women, a patriarchal imposition on their ambitions, and a source of profound inequity. But is this attitude accurate? Do women *want* to be working more, if only the kids—and their useless husbands—would let them? And do we know that more government support would enable them to do so and close the wage gap?

Actually, there is no evidence for either of these propositions. If women work fewer hours than men do, it appears to be because they want it that way. About two-thirds of the part-time workforce in the United States is female. According to a 2007 Pew Research survey, only 21 percent of working mothers with minor children want to be in the office full time. Sixty percent say that they would prefer to work part time, and 19 percent would like to give up their jobs altogether. For working fathers, the numbers are reversed: 72 percent want to work full time and 12 percent part time.

In fact, women choose fewer hours—despite the resulting gap in earnings—all over the world. That includes countries with generous family leave and child care policies. Look at

Iceland, recently crowned the world's most egalitarian nation by the World Economic Forum. The country boasts a female prime minister, a law requiring that the boards of midsize and larger businesses be at least 40 percent female, excellent public child care, and a family leave policy that would make NOW members swoon. Yet despite successful efforts to get men to take paternity leave, Icelandic women still take considerably more time off than men do. They also are far more likely to work part time. According to the Organisation for Economic Co-operation and Development (OECD), this queen of women-friendly countries has a bigger wage gap—women make 62 percent of what men do—than the United States does.

Sweden, in many people's minds the world's gender utopia, also has a de facto mommy track. Sweden has one of the highest proportions of working women in the world and a commitment to gender parity that's close to a national religion. In addition to child care, the country offers paid parental leave that includes two months specifically reserved for fathers. Yet moms still take four times as much leave as dads do. (Women are also more likely to be in lower-paid public-sector jobs; according to sociologist Linda Haas, Sweden has "one of the most sex-segregated labor markets in the world.")

Far more women than men work part time; almost *half* of all mothers are on the job 30 hours a week or less. The gender wage gap among full-time workers in Sweden is 15 percent. That's lower than in the United States, at least according to the flawed data we have, but it's hardly the feminist Promised Land.

The list goes on. In the Netherlands, over 70 percent of women work part time and say that they want it that way. According to the Netherlands Institute for Social Research, surveys found that only 4 percent of female part-timers wish that they had full-time jobs. In the United Kingdom, half of female GPs work part time, and the National Health Service is scrambling to cope with a dearth of doctor hours. Interestingly enough, countries with higher GDPs tend to have the highest percentage of women in part-time work. In fact, the OECD reports that in many of its richest countries, including Denmark, Sweden, Iceland, Germany, the U.K., and the U.S., the percentage of the female workforce in part-time positions has gone *up* over the last decade.

So it makes no sense to think of either the mommy track or the resulting wage differential as an injustice to women. Less time at work, whether in the form of part-time jobs or fewer full-time hours, is what many women want and what those who can afford it tend to choose. Feminists can object till the singularity arrives that women are "socialized" to think that they have to be the primary parent. But after decades of feminism and Nordic engineering, the continuing female tropism toward shorter work hours suggests that that view is either false or irrelevant. Even the determined Swedes haven't been able to get women to stick around the office.

That doesn't mean that the mommy track doesn't present a problem, particularly in a culture in which close to half of all marriages break down. A woman can have a baby, decide to reduce her hours and her pay, forgo a pension, and then, ten years later, watch her husband run off with the Pilates instructor. The problem isn't what it used to be when women had fewer degrees and less work experience during their childless years; women today are in better shape to jump-start their careers if need be. The risk remains, however.

It's not at all clear how to solve this problem or even if there is a solution, especially during these fiscally challenged days. But one thing is clear: The wage-gap debate ought to begin with the mommy track, not with proofy statistics.

"When we see our male CEOs taking off a day to care for a sick child, then we will be working in a more gender-equal workplace—and a more gender-equal world."

The Gender Pay Gap Is Falling for Young Women

Hope Yen

Hope Yen is a national reporter for the Associated Press. In the following viewpoint, she says that a Pew Research Center report shows that women are making gains in terms of pay in comparison to men. However, she says, women still see inequality in the workplace and still have not reached equal footing with male counterparts in high-level jobs. Yen suggests that this continuing inequality may be linked to the fact that women make more work sacrifices for children and family than do men.

As you read, consider the following questions:

1. How do women's college completion rates compare to those of men, and how has this affected the gender pay gap, according to Yen?

Hope Yen, "Pay Gains for Young Women; Inequality Still Seen," Associated Press, December 11, 2013. AP.org. © 2013 Associated Press. Reproduced by permission.

2. Who is Mary Barra, and why is her achievement significant?

3. According to Yen, what percentage of women versus what percentage of men report that being a working parent makes it difficult to advance in a job?

Young American women are increasingly likely to receive pay nearly equal to their male counterparts, with earnings at 93 percent of men, a new study finds. Still, those women remain as pessimistic as their mothers and grandmothers regarding gender equality.

A Mixed Picture

A report for release Wednesday [in December 2013] by the Pew Research Center paints a mixed picture.

While women under 32 now have higher rates of college completion than men that age, the analysis of census and labor data shows their hourly earnings will slip further behind by the women's mid-30s, if the experience of the past three decades is a guide.

That widening gap is due in part to the many women who take time off or reduce their hours to start families. Other factors cited in the report are gender stereotyping, discrimination, weaker professional networks and women's hesitancy to aggressively push for raises and promotions, which together may account for 20 to 40 percent of the pay gap.

In all, 75 percent of women ages 18–32 say the U.S. needs to do more to bring about equality in the workplace, a percentage similar to baby boomer women ages 49–67 and higher than other age groups. Some 57 percent of young men answered that way.

Even so, just 15 percent of young women say they have been discriminated against because of their gender.

"Today's generation of young women is entering the labor force near parity with men in terms of earnings and extremely well prepared in terms of their educational attainment," said Kim Parker, associate director with the Pew Social & Demographic Trends Project. "They feel empowered in many ways, yet when they look at the workplace, they see it as a 'man's world' with the deck stacked against them."

"They think that men earn more than women for doing the same job and that it's easier for men to get top executive jobs than it is for women," she said.

Women are increasingly moving into higher career positions both in government and business. They make up nearly half the workforce, and the share of women in managerial and administrative occupations is nearly equal to that of men—15 percent compared to 17 percent. Another landmark came Tuesday, when General Motors [Company] picked Mary Barra, a 33-year company veteran, as the first female head of a major U.S. car company. Still, women currently hold just 4.5 percent of Fortune 1000 CEO [chief executive officer] positions, the Pew report said.

Andrew Cherlin, a sociology professor at Johns Hopkins University, attributed young women's negative assessments about gender equality to their rising career expectations. "More doors are now open to women, but they can now see how far they are from equality in high-level jobs," he said.

Near-Equal Pay

The near-equal pay for young women is being driven in large part by their educational gains. Some 38 percent of women ages 25–32 now hold bachelor's degrees, compared to 31 percent of young men. As a result, 49 percent of employed workers with at least a bachelor's degree last year were women, up from 36 percent in 1980. That means more women in higher-skilled, higher-paying positions.

The current ratio of hourly earnings for young women to young men, now at 93 percent, is up from 67 percent in 1980 and is the highest in government records dating back to at least 1979. Across all age groups, the median hourly wage for women last year was 84 percent as much as men—$14.90 vs. $17.79, up from 64 percent in 1980.

At the same time, the Pew study indicates that a woman's job advancement often will hit a ceiling, due in part to competing demands of work and family. Women remain twice as likely as men to work part time and are more likely to take significant time off from employment during their lives to care for children or other family members.

Among young women, 59 percent say that being a working parent makes it harder to advance in a job or career, compared to just 19 percent of young men. Across all age groups, 22 percent of women and 9 percent of men report having quit jobs for family reasons at some point during their working lives.

Fewer young women than young men aspire to become a boss or top manager. Some 34 percent say they're not interested, compared to 24 percent of young men. And the vast majority of adults of all ages who reduced their work hours to care for family members—94 percent—say they are glad they did it.

"This report shows that we are still very much in a 'stalled revolution' when it comes to gender equality in the workplace—and young women see it," said Pamela Smock, a sociology professor at the University of Michigan. "When we see our male CEOs taking off a day to care for a sick child, then we will be working in a more gender-equal workplace—and a more gender-equal world."

The Pew study was based on interviews with 2,002 adults by cell phone or landline from Oct. 7 to 27 [2013]. The Pew poll has a margin of error of plus or minus 2.7 percentage points.

| *"For advocates for women and minority workers, the mood is mostly dispirited."*

It Is Harder to Fight Workplace Discrimination Today

Nina Martin

Nina Martin is a journalist at ProPublica, covering issues of gender and sexuality. In the following viewpoint, she reports on the changes in class-action discrimination lawsuits following the Supreme Court decision in Wal-Mart Stores, Inc. v. Dukes. *The court made it much more difficult to bring class-action lawsuits, and as a result, the number of lawsuits brought and damages awarded have dropped. Plaintiffs continue to try to bring class-action suits, but their claims must be more focused, and the cases are more difficult to win. Martin argues that this makes it harder for women and minorities to sue to end discriminatory practices in the workplace.*

As you read, consider the following questions:

1. What evidence does Martin cite to show how the *Dukes* ruling has reshaped the legal landscape?

Nina Martin, "The Impact and Echoes of the Wal-Mart Discrimination Case," ProPublica, September 27, 2013. www.propublica.org. © 2013 ProPublica. Reproduced by permission.

2. According to the viewpoint, who is Edith Arana?

3. According to the viewpoint, what is the Nucor lawsuit, and how was it affected by the *Dukes* ruling?

When the U.S. Supreme Court issued its 5–4 decision in *Wal-Mart [Stores, Inc.] v. Dukes* in June 2011, no one needed a Richter scale to know it was a big one. In throwing out a mammoth lawsuit by women employees who claimed that they'd been systematically underpaid and underpromoted by the world's biggest corporation, the ruling upended decades of employment discrimination law and raised serious barriers to future large-scale discrimination cases of every kind.

Setbacks for Women and Minorities

Employers rejoiced. Others predicted serious setbacks for women and minorities, especially in employment discrimination cases brought under Title VII of the Civil Rights Act of 1964. That landmark law had opened the way to the use of the class-action lawsuit as a potent weapon for people who could not stand up for their rights on their own.

Two years later, it's becoming clear just how much the ruling has reshaped the American legal landscape.

The *Dukes* decision has already been cited more than 1,200 times in rulings by federal and state courts, a figure seen by experts as remarkable. Jury verdicts have been overturned, settlements thrown out, and class actions rejected or decertified, in many instances undoing years of litigation. The rulings have come in every part of the country, in lawsuits involving all types of companies, including retailers (Family Dollar Stores), government contractors (Lockheed Martin Corp.), business-services providers (Cintas Corp.), and magazines (Hearst Corp.). The aftershocks have been felt in many kinds of lawsuits beyond the employment field as well.

Many of the rulings since 2011 have not been surprising. Some have been relatively narrow. But others have tread into unexpected territory.

This past August [2013], for example, a federal appeals court in Philadelphia upheld the dismissal of a $7 million settlement between the former National City Bank and 153,000 black and Hispanic borrowers who claimed that the bank had discriminated against them in how it charged mortgage points and fees during the housing bubble. Neither side had sought to revisit the 2010 accord, but the courts did so anyway, ruling that because the class action probably wouldn't have been certified under *Dukes*, the settlement was suspect, too.

"That is pretty extraordinary," said Gerald Maatman Jr. of Seyfarth Shaw in Chicago, one of the leading law firms in the country defending businesses and employers against class actions. "It shows how much the standards have changed."

Courts in prior decades had typically rubber-stamped such settlements, he said.

"It's a whole new world," Maatman said.

One measure of that change is the difference in the size of employee discrimination settlements as reported in Maatman's widely read *Workplace Class Action Blog*. In 2010, the year before the *Dukes* decision, the top 10 settlements totaled $346 million; in 2012, the first year after *Dukes*, that total plummeted 87 percent, to $45 million.

Another measure, lawyers representing women and minorities say, is the drop-off in new employment discrimination class-action lawsuits being filed. Before *Dukes*, it was normal to see 25 or 30 such cases every year, said Jocelyn Larkin, executive director of the Impact Fund, a law firm/national litigation resource center based in Berkeley, Calif. . . . Now, Larkin said, the number of new cases is closer to 10 or 12 a year.

Even in this new world, there have been some class-action victories. On Sept. 6, Bank of America and its Merrill Lynch unit settled a sex discrimination class action with female brokers for $39 million. The week before, Merrill agreed to pay another $160 million for discriminating against African-American brokers, the largest class-action settlement ever in a race-bias case. Merrill and Bank of America had tried to argue that the *Wal-Mart* ruling meant that the lawsuits should not be allowed to proceed as class actions—an argument that, in these instances, a federal court didn't buy.

But for advocates for women and minority workers, the mood is mostly dispirited. Economic disparities—between people of color and whites and between men and women—have been widening and complaints of mistreatment in the workplace are common. San Francisco's Equal Rights Advocates, another firm involved in the *Dukes* case, has seen a tripling of calls to its nationwide hotline, said executive director Noreen Farrell. Many of the calls are from low-wage women facing discrimination on the job and elsewhere.

Even before *Dukes*, "they already had many obstacles," Farrell said. To fight these battles individually, "it's often impossible."

Wal-Mart and Discrimination

Edith Arana, now in her early 50s, was a mother of five with 10 years of retail experience when she started working at a Duarte, Calif., Wal-Mart store in the 1990s for $7 an hour. In six years, she received excellent performance reviews but never rose beyond a low-level "support manager." When she began pressing for a promotion, her supervisors cut her hours, she claimed, finally forcing her out of her job.

"I thought to myself, no one's going to believe you—you're just one person," Arana said.

Eventually, though, Arana found her way to Equal Rights Advocates. The firm had heard many similar stories. Their lawsuit was filed in San Francisco in 2001.

Wal-Mart had a written antidiscrimination policy and insisted that it "does not condone discrimination of any kind."

It also noted that "women hold positions of significant responsibility" at the company. But it left most employment decisions to the discretion of local managers at thousands of stores across the country. That led to systemic discrimination, the women and their lawyers claimed. Wal-Mart's own wage and promotion data seemed to show pronounced, persistent wage disparities between male and female employees at every level, from hourly workers to senior managers.

"Wal-Mart has had a strong policy against discrimination in place for many years and we continue to be a great place for women to work and advance," the company said in a statement to ProPublica.

"The opportunities left a lot of discretion to managers to make decisions based on their own personal views and predilections and idiosyncrasies and biases," said Joseph M. Sellers, a partner at the Washington, D.C., firm Cohen Milstein who eventually helped argue the case before the Supreme Court.

It was a theory that had underpinned many successful employment discrimination cases over the last 50 years. In 2004, the federal judge overseeing the case certified it as the largest sex and employment discrimination class action in U.S. history. The Ninth Circuit Court of Appeals twice affirmed that ruling.

The Supreme Court ultimately thought otherwise. In his opinion, Justice Antonin Scalia rejected the notion that such a vast company should be held responsible for the workplace decisions of thousands of local managers exercising their own discretion, even if those actions ended up having a disparate impact on female employees.

"What the Supreme Court said is that you can't group dozens and dozens of different classes into one class action and say, 'Oh everyone's an employee and everyone's fighting gender discrimination, so they belong together,'" said Ted Frank, an adjunct fellow with the Manhattan Institute's Center for Legal Policy.

Other experts blamed the plaintiffs for overreaching, and in the process inviting a more conservative Supreme Court to register one of its most significant pro-business rulings.

"When plaintiffs seek to maximize their leverage by suing on a company-wide, 'mega' basis, they invite judicial reversal," Columbia law professor John Coffee wrote soon after the decision. "Hubris leads to disaster, and *Wal-Mart* presents the paradigmatic case of such a train wreck."

Other aspects of the ruling were also far-reaching. In particular, the court rejected a 35-year-old framework for calculating monetary damages in employment discrimination class actions. Instead of using a statistical formula that assessed damages for the whole class, plaintiffs now had to have individual trials. Many lawyers didn't see this coming, especially when liberal justices joined conservatives to make that part of the ruling unanimous.

One predictable casualty was the *Dukes* case itself. This August, the San Francisco federal judge overseeing the lawsuit concluded that even a scaled-back version of the lawsuit, covering only Wal-Mart workers in California, could not move forward. A Texas judge said the same thing last fall about a version of the suit filed there.

Arana, one of the original plaintiffs, lamented the clear implications for female workers like her.

"It can't just be you out there," Arana said. "No one person, no one attorney, no one support system is enough."

Wal-Mart, in its statement, said: "The allegations from these five plaintiffs are not representative of the positive experiences that hundreds of thousands of women have had working at Wal-Mart."

New Uncertainty

Beyond *Dukes*, the greatest disruption has been to what are sometimes called "legacy cases"—the sizable and often significant class-action lawsuits that began before *Dukes* was de-

Betty Dukes and Wal-Mart

Betty Dukes, for her part, eventually got a real raise. In 2002 she heard that two male greeters, one brand-new to the company, were earning more than she was. Wal-Mart's database, which the [*Wal-Mart Stores Inc. v. Dukes*] legal team now has in its possession, confirmed the break-room gossip: The new greeter made more than $9 per hour, while Dukes's wage was $8.47. The . . . lawyers filed an additional charge of sex discrimination against the company on her behalf. In March 2003, Wal-Mart gave Betty Dukes a raise, calling it an "internal equity adjustment," and she's now making over $10 an hour. It was her biggest raise in her history with the company. "They're trying to clean up," says the plaintiffs' lead counsel, Brad Seligman, and adds with a grin, "I'm sure it has absolutely nothing to do with the case!"

There's almost no doubt that Dukes wouldn't have gotten this raise without the lawsuit. She feels strongly, though, that her raise should be just the beginning of Wal-Mart's reforms. The company needs to change its treatment of all women, not just her. Besides, $10 an hour is still a lot less than Dukes would be making if she were promoted. "I'm still living far below the poverty line," she points out. "That ten dollars doesn't allow me to have my own place."

Liza Featherstone, Selling Women Short:
The Landmark Battle for Workers' Rights at Wal-Mart.
New York: Basic Books, 2004.

cided. The fate of a race discrimination lawsuit against a South Carolina steel factory owned by Nucor Corp. is one example of the ripple effects of the *Dukes* decision.

The lawsuit, brought by seven black Nucor employees in 2004 on behalf of more than 100 coworkers, alleged a widespread pattern of racist acts and promotion practices at the factory. White supervisors and employees reportedly referred to their black colleagues as "yard apes" and "porch monkeys." Racial epithets were supposedly broadcast over the plant-wide radio system, along with "Dixie," "High Cotton" and monkey noises in response to the communications of black workers. The lawsuit said the Confederate flag was displayed throughout the plant and even emblazoned next to Nucor's logo on items sold in the plant's gift shop. Yet another allegation was that whites circulated emails showing black people with nooses around their necks.

In court documents, Nucor denied the allegations and said that all employment decisions were made for "legitimate, nondiscriminatory business reasons."

In nine years, courts have weighed in at least seven times on whether the case should be certified as a class action, with the Fourth Circuit Court of Appeals in Richmond—not known for being particularly sympathetic to workers—finally deciding that there was ample evidence to let the case proceed as a class action. Then, after *Dukes*, the class was again decertified for all claims except hostile work environment; earlier this month [September 2013], Nucor's lawyers were once again in court arguing that even that limited class action should be thrown out because most of the alleged racist acts were limited to one department.

"The problem with the length of this case is that as the case goes on, the Supreme Court keeps drilling more nails into the coffin of effective civil rights law," said Armand Derfner, a Charleston, S.C., lawyer representing the workers. "The practical effect of decertification is that even if we win, there will not be the kind of change that Title VII was designed to create. A handful of people will win," but the company "won't have to make fundamental changes that they don't want to make."

For all of its force, the *Dukes* decision contained some ambiguity as well. For instance, the decision said that for a class-action lawsuit to proceed, plaintiffs would now have to show "significant proof of a general policy of discrimination" on the part of the employer. What exactly constituted "a general policy" was left unclear.

"The ruling used some new language which nobody quite knew what it meant," said Joseph Sellers, the Washington lawyer who had helped argue the *Dukes* case. "This has injected a new level of uncertainty into cases that were already challenging and expensive and time-consuming to bring."

The uncertainty spawned by the *Dukes* decision has been compounded by other Supreme Court decisions. All of it has left plaintiffs trying to "reboot" their various cases with new arguments, and defense lawyers responding with "novel" theories of their own, said Maatman, the Chicago lawyer who represents employers. And many lawyers on both sides are watching to see if the *Dukes* decision gets invoked in major pending cases, including a class-action lawsuit brought against BP for the 2010 Deepwater Horizon drilling disaster in the Gulf of Mexico.

Class Action Goes Forward

The explicit and enduring ramifications of *Dukes*, then, are still to be determined.

"We're still seeing employee class actions—those haven't died," said Ted Frank of the Manhattan Institute. "We're seeing consumer class actions and securities class actions—those haven't died. Certainly some bad class actions were slapped down, but the legitimate class actions are going forward."

Indeed, in perhaps the biggest victory for workers in the post-*Dukes* era, the Seventh Circuit Court of Appeals in Chicago last year refused to throw out the 2005 lawsuit brought by George McReynolds and other black brokers against Merrill Lynch—the case that led to the record $160 million settlement. Writing for a three-judge panel, Judge Richard Posner, a conservative who has displayed a fierce independent streak as well as a willingness to clash with Justice Scalia in a number of recent writings, said Merrill Lynch's pay and promotion policies were fundamentally different from Wal-Mart's in how they encouraged systematic bias.

The *McReynolds* ruling [referring to the ruling in *McReynolds v. Merrill Lynch*], then, shows one possible way forward for employees and their lawyers, Maatman said.

"You're seeing plaintiffs' lawyers recalibrate, making classes much smaller, focusing on an issue that might be doable on a class-wide basis, not trying to certify, as they did in *Dukes*, the whole enchilada," he said.

Perhaps the next high-profile test of this strategy will come in March 2014 in San Francisco, where [Barack] Obama appointee Edward Chen—formerly an ACLU [American Civil Liberties Union] attorney specializing in discrimination cases, and now, after a two-year confirmation battle, a U.S. district judge—is set to preside in a trial against Costco and its promotion policies. Citing *McReynolds*, Chen ruled in 2012 that the sex discrimination suit, brought by 700 of the retailer's female workers, could move forward as a class.

In the post-*Dukes* world, "there's trepidation," acknowledged Emily Martin, vice president and general counsel for the National Women's Law Center, which has been closely monitoring the case and its aftermath. "But it's not as though everyone is rolling up their tents and going home."

"Now a court of law . . . said you can be fired if your boss thinks you're too good-looking."

Being "Too Beautiful" Becomes On-Job Liability

Caryl Rivers and Rosalind C. Barnett

Caryl Rivers and Rosalind C. Barnett are the authors of The New Soft War on Women: How the Myth of Female Ascendance Is Hurting Women, Men—and Our Economy. *In the following viewpoint, they report on a July 2013 ruling by the Iowa Supreme Court that determined that a boss was allowed to fire a female subordinate because he feared that he would be tempted to have an affair with her, thus damaging his marriage. The authors say that this is a clear example of discrimination and opens the door for women to be fired at any time for no cause. They say that the ruling is part of a broader pattern of discrimination in the workplace where women's appearances are constantly held up to scrutiny and used as a way to harass them and discriminate against them.*

As you read, consider the following questions:

1. According to an Iowa district court, why was dental assistant Melissa Nelson fired?

2. According to Debrahlee Lorenzana, what sort of harassment did she experience at work?

3. What do the authors say that women need to overcome discrimination at work?

Are you "too beautiful" to be in the workplace? Can your boss fire you if he thinks your appearance is a threat to his marriage?

The answer, at least according to the Iowa Supreme Court, is "yes."

Here's just another obstacle to women's advancement in the workplace; one of many that we argue create a new "soft war" on women.

Research finds that women are penalized if they are seen as too talkative, too competent, too aggressive, too self-promoting—or, ironically, too passive—too self-effacing or not caring enough.

Now, a court of law on July 17 said you can be fired if your boss thinks you're too good-looking.

This case arose when a 33-year-old dental assistant, Melissa Nelson, was fired by her boss, dentist James Knight of Fort Dodge, because he believed her good looks were a threat to his marriage. He said he would be tempted to begin an affair with her.

Nelson reportedly engaged in no improper behavior. It was just that her boss believed that he could not control his own sexual feelings, and so he had the right to deprive her of her livelihood.

This notion would be laughable, except that when Nelson brought suit for sex discrimination, an Iowa district court dismissed the case.

Amazingly, it found that she was fired "not because of her gender but because she was a threat to the marriage of Dr. Knight."

When she appealed, the Iowa Supreme Court said the key issue was "whether an employee who has not engaged in flirtatious conduct may be lawfully terminated simply because the boss views the employee as an irresistible attraction." The court ruled that the answer was yes.

Similar Case

Appearance was also a factor when a banker sued Citibank in 2010 for firing her because she was too curvy. Debrahlee Lorenzana, an attractive young Puerto Rican woman, was hired to be a business banker at a New York Citibank branch office.

She said her male managers gave her a list of clothing items she was not allowed to wear: turtlenecks, pencil skirts, fitted suits and three-inch heels.

According to her lawsuit, her bosses told her that "as a result of the shape of her figure, such clothes were purportedly 'too distracting' for her male colleagues and supervisors to bear."

After trying to dress more conservatively, which included wearing no makeup, she was told she looked "sickly," and when she left her hair curly instead of straightening it, they told her she should go ahead and straighten it every day.

She finally got the message that there was no way she could win. "I could have worn a paper bag, and it would not have mattered," she told the *Village Voice*. "If it wasn't my shirt, it was my pants. If it wasn't my pants, it was my shoes. They picked on me every single day." (The case went to arbitration; the results were not publicly revealed.)

What's the message here? Women can't win. They are constantly inundated by media advertising, telling them that, above all, they must be attractive and pleasing to men. But at the same time, they must be supercompetent to succeed on the job.

A woman has absolutely no power to control how her employer will see her. Her behavior can be irreproachable and her competence unquestioned. But if her boss decides he can't handle his feelings, she's toast. The onus is not on him to keep his personal feelings under control, which we are all expected to do at work. Why is his concern about his marriage her problem?

'Classic Discrimination'

Why did an all-male court not recognize that in the Nelson case, the dentist's behavior was classic discrimination?

Should the law really allow men to fire perfectly qualified women when they perceive a threat to their marriages?

If this precedent is allowed to stand, male managers will be given broad license to fire women for all kinds of reasons. Suppose a male manager is in fact threatened by a highly competent female employee who might be after his job. All he has to say, with no proof, is that he feels she's a threat to his marriage, and so he can fire her. Under this interpretation of the law, she has no recourse.

What if the situation were reversed? What if a female manager felt that her attractive male assistant was a threat to her marriage and fired him? Can you imagine a male court upholding that decision?

Women are expected to keep their emotions in check at work and if they don't, they are seen as a problem. But men can let their feelings determine their actions, with no penalty. For example, male managers who display anger are not evaluated poorly by their coworkers, but angry women are seen as incompetent and out of control.

Women are being urged to live up to their potential, get as much education as they can and "lean in" to their careers, as

Facebook executive Sheryl Sandberg puts it in her best-selling book. But new obstacles keep surfacing where we least expect them.

Women can't keep leaping all these hurdles on their own. The courts need to be allies of women's rights in the workplace, not just another barrier to their success. We'll never win the "soft war" unless things change.

Periodical and Internet Sources Bibliography

The following articles have been selected to supplement the diverse views presented in this chapter.

Jillian Berman	"At This Rate, Women Won't Make as Much as Men for at Least 75 Years," *Huffington Post*, July 15, 2014.
Paula J. Caplan	"Women as Subjects of Employment Discrimination," *Psychology Today*, December 29, 2013.
Simon Goodley	"Gender Pay Gap: Female Bosses Earn 35% Less than Male Colleagues," *Guardian*, August 18, 2014.
Vivien Labaton	"Five Myths About the Gender Pay Gap," *Washington Post*, July 25, 2014.
Meredith Lepore	"Pretty Woman: Are Your Looks Hurting Your Career?," Levo League, March 20, 2013.
Lisa M. Maatz	"The Awful Truth Behind the Gender Pay Gap," *Forbes*, April 7, 2014.
Jena McGregor	"Young Women Are Closing the Pay Gap," *Washington Post*, December 11, 2013.
Claire Cain Miller	"Pay Gap Is Because of Gender, Not Jobs," *New York Times*, April 24, 2014.
Colleen McCain Nelson	"Poll: Most Women See Bias in the Workplace," *Wall Street Journal*, April 12, 2013.
Ben Waber	"What Data Analytics Says About Gender Inequality in the Workplace," *Bloomberg Businessweek*, January 30, 2014.
Anna Williams	"Why Good Looks Could Be a Career Liability," LearnVest, July 18, 2013.

OPPOSING
VIEWPOINTS®
SERIES

CHAPTER 2

How Does Motherhood Affect Working Women?

Chapter Preface

The Pew Research Center reports that since the start of the recession in 2007, the amount of mothers working full time has increased significantly. However, both parents working full time creates a dilemma of what to do about child care. According to Child Care Aware of America, nearly eleven million children younger than five years old, whose parents are working, are in a child care setting, spending on average thirty-six hours a week in child care.

Child care in the United States is poorly monitored and can be substandard and even dangerous, argues Jonathan Cohn in an article for the *New Republic* on April 15, 2013. Cohn points to a deadly fire at Jackie's Child Care, a center illegally run by Jessica Tata, a woman with a criminal record. According to Cohn, of the millions of children who are in the care of someone other than a parent,

> Most of them are in centers, although a sizable minority attend home day cares like the one run by Jessica Tata. In other countries, such services are subsidized and well-regulated. In the United States, despite the fact that work and family life has changed profoundly in recent decades, we lack anything resembling an actual child care system. Excellent day cares are available, of course, if you have the money to pay for them and the luck to secure a spot.

Jessica Grose writing for *Slate* on April 15, 2013, points out that the problem is not just dangerous conditions at some day cares, but routine lack of affordable quality day care for large numbers of families. Grose explains that "only 10 percent of children receive 'high quality' day care. . . . The median yearly salary for day care workers is less than $20,000. Day care is more expensive than rent for families in 22 states." Grose points out that France is often held up as a counterexample; France has "inexpensive municipal day care" and "universal free preschool beginning at age 3." It also pays child care workers very well compared to American workers. Grose suggests that one way to move toward a French system of child care would be to increase the number of children per worker in US day cares, allowing greater pay for workers and improving quality of care.

Whatever the solution, however, it is clear that the lack of affordable, quality care options makes balancing work and family more difficult for parents, especially for women who remain disproportionately tasked with child care duties.

The authors of the viewpoints in the following chapter examine other issues concerning working mothers, including whether maternity leave helps or hurts working mothers and whether mothers who work are happier and healthier than their stay-at-home counterparts.

> "Every few months, it seems, researchers unveil more proof that working moms are happier than stay-at-home moms."

Moms Who Work Are Happier and Healthier

Lisa Belkin

Lisa Belkin is a senior columnist for life, work, and family at the Huffington Post. In the following viewpoint, she reports on a study that shows that women who work outside the home are happier and healthier than those who are stay-at-home mothers. She adds, however, that such studies do little to help provide women with choices about child care and working. She suggests that expanding options for all women is a more important goal than determining which moms are the most relatively happy.

As you read, consider the following questions:

1. What are two studies that Belkin cites to show that moms who work are relatively happy compared to moms who don't?

2. Why does Belkin say that the "mommy wars" are a fight that no one can win?

3. What kind of study does Belkin say she wishes she could see?

Every few months, it seems, researchers unveil more proof that working moms are happier than stay-at-home moms. And every few months, the same old debate erupts as a result over whether that can possibly be true.

Let's make this time different.

More Energy, Less Depression

The most recent study was presented this weekend [in August 2012] at the American Sociological Association meeting in Denver, where researchers from the University of Akron and Penn State University told us that mothers who go back to work within weeks of giving birth had "more energy, mobility, and less depression by age 40" than those who spend months or years at home.

That comes on the heels of a Gallup study in May, which found stay-at-home mothers were more likely to experience stress, worry, anger and sadness than were those who held paying jobs. Among the findings: 28 percent of the at-home moms described themselves as depressed, compared with 17 percent of employed moms.

A few days earlier, the British *Journal of Epidemiology and Community Health* reported that "housewives" were more likely to be obese (38 percent) than were those who juggled children, a steady relationship and a paycheck (23 percent).

And in December of last year, the *Journal of Family Psychology* in the U.S. concluded that a 10-year-long study following new mothers found that those who held a paying job, whether full time or part time, were in better health in general, and less depressed in particular, than those who did not.

"Yet Another Mommy Wars Study" was how the website Mommyish described the latest report.

"From the Mommy Wars . . ." began the headline on Forbes.com.

Life Ratings and Positive Emotions, by Motherhood Status

	Stay-at-home moms	Employed moms	Employed women (No child at home)
Thriving	55%	63%	61%
Struggling	42%	36%	38%
Suffering	3%	1%	2%
Smiled or laughed a lot	81%	86%	85%
Learned something interesting	61%	66%	67%
Experienced enjoyment	81%	86%	86%
Experienced happiness	86%	91%	90%

Jan. 1–April 30, 2012,
Gallup-Healthways Well-Being Index.

TAKEN FROM: Hanna Brooks Olsen, "Working Moms Have Awesome Lives, Are Way Less Depressed than Stay-at-Home Moms," Blisstree, May 18, 2012.

Yes, it is tempting to see all this as a trope from an ongoing conflict. "It's okay if I leave my children with a caregiver and go to work because staying home is just making you fat and depressed," employed mothers get to say. Then we all go back to our stations and prepare for the next chance to prove that "my choice is better than yours."

That would make sense if this were a fight that someone could actually "win," with one side bringing the other around. In other words, if this were a question of "which is better for Mom," then new mothers could look at all this data and make a logical choice.

Not a Real Choice

But this is not a question of logic, or, necessarily, real choice. If women stayed home (or went to work) specifically because they thought it would make them happier (or thinner), then these studies serve their purpose. I would argue, though, that depression and the like is a side effect of decisions reached for reasons that have little or nothing to do with whether a woman will be happy.

Happiness (and fulfillment and self-worth) are part of these choices, of course. But the real roots here are far more likely to be money (the decision to go to work and earn some, or to stay home and not pay a caregiver) and welfare of children (the belief that a child will benefit from the presence of a parent, or the role model of a working one) and the realities of the workplace (the availability of employment for both spouses and the reality that if one must work extreme hours in order to keep a job that leaves the other to carry the home front).

Telling those who choose home, therefore, that "studies show you will be less depressed if you choose otherwise" doesn't make a different choice possible.

In an ideal world, there would be fewer studies about relative happiness and more about what could be done to maximize happiness for both "camps." Studies of how to provide more mental health treatment for poorer women, who are more likely to be part of the depressed stay-at-home cohort. How to improve the availability of child care for women who would like to work but can't find safe affordable placement for their children. How to increase flexibility in the workplace, so that the choice isn't keep the job or be home for dinner.

And while I am making my wish list, I would like one more thing: a study or two about whether men who stay home are more or less depressed than those who don't.

Leaving them out of this conversation is getting depressing.

"I'm not saying guilt is good; it's not, but denying its very existence puts women into categories—again."

Working Mothers Are Guilty, but Not Unhappy

Office Mum

Office Mum is a blog that is written about work and family issues. In the following viewpoint, the author responds to a survey that shows that working mothers do not feel guilty. She says that this survey does not conform to her experiences. Many women do feel guilty in trying to balance work and motherhood she says, although that does not mean working mothers feel unhappy. She argues that acknowledging guilt is important so that working mothers who do feel guilty do not think they are doing something wrong.

As you read, consider the following questions:

1. Why does the author say she doesn't buy the argument that working women feel no guilt?

2. According to the viewpoint, guilt doesn't mean wrong-doing; what does it mean instead in this context?

"Mythbusting the Mythbusters on Working Mother Guilt," *Office Mum*, May 14, 2014. Officemum.ie. © 2014 Office Mum. Reproduced by permission.

3. What term does the author say she is going to use instead of "guilt," and why?

Working mother guilt is a myth, according to widely publicised survey findings from UK [United Kingdom] parenting website Mumsnet.

No Guilt?

48% of the 900 mothers polled said that they were happier having a job than being at home, sparking a range of newspaper articles on the topic, including this one by Bryony Gordon who said:

"The idea that working women feel guilty about not staying at home to look after their children has this week been blown apart, proved to be nothing more than a great big myth."

According to an article in Herald.ie, "On online forums and blogs mothers have been telling each other that they don't actually feel guilty about going to work."

The *Telegraph* reports "the idea that working mothers feel guilty about not staying at home to look after their children is a myth, new research has suggested."

I just don't buy it.

It's a few weeks since I read the articles, but they really caught my attention. The conclusion goes against everything I've experienced myself and everything I've heard in the many, many conversations that I've had in real life and online with mothers.

Every working mother I've ever spoken to experiences guilt to some extent, at least some of the time. Of course not all the time—we're not sitting at our desks, crying into the famously hot tea that we've waited throughout maternity leave to try. We're not agonising over whether or not we should even *be* at work while sitting through a meeting. At work, we're mostly busy focusing on—well—work.

The reality, as far as I can see, is that most of us like working, while at the same time, most of us wish we had more time with our kids.

The guilt kicks in when a baby is sick soon after starting crèche [day care center]; when a toddler cries during morning drop-off, or when homework time is snappish because it's 7 o'clock and both parent and child are just too tired.

Guilt can sidle up beside us when we're sitting down at night; reading an article about children doing better at something if they have a parent looking after them full time, or an online discussion about how lovely it is to be at home with them when they're young.

Questions, doubts, insecurities creep in. A little gut-twist by the too-close-for-comfort uninvited guest—a moment wondering "what if I regret this?"

And then we click to the next article (which says kids do better at something if they go to crèche) or change the conversation and move on. Guilt pushed away until the next time.

And this is a generalisation of course—some mothers feel guilt much more forcefully than others, and some not at all. But the Mumsnet findings also spawned generalisations— blanket claims that working mother guilt is a myth. Just like that.

Nothing Wrong with Guilt

It shouldn't really matter, but I really needed to work out for myself what was prompting the black-and-white views held by the various writers—the unquestioning belief that the survey results are true, and the assumption that they're speaking on behalf of all of us.

A survey of 900 women surely doesn't represent the entire world of working mothers, and eradicate the concept of working mother guilt with the click of a mouse? I'm not saying guilt is good, it's not, but denying its very existence puts

Guilt Is Good

Bottom line, if you're a mom, you'll feel guilty all the time, and this is true because you're a daughter as well, and God only knows how many times you failed your poor mother.

Shame on you, and guilt, too.

Now, to come to my point. If you think I'm going to preach to you that guilt is a bad thing, you're wrong.

I don't want you to change.

Because I like you just the way you are.

Don't lose your guilt. Embrace it, like me.

I don't feel guilty for feeling guilty.

I've long ago accepted that guilt is a part of me, like cellulite.

Guilt makes me work harder, do more errands, and get to the dry cleaners before closing.

Guilt means I'm always early, everywhere.

Guilt makes me pay my bills on time.

Guilt makes me nicer to people.

Guilt helps me be a better mother.

Guilt gets me on the elliptical. Occasionally, but only on Level One.

Guilt makes the journey of life into one long guilt trip. But in a nice way.

Lisa Scottoline and Francesca Serritella,
Have a Nice Guilt Trip.
New York: St. Martin's Press, 2014.

women into categories—again. It leaves the reader thinking "Oh, but I do feel guilty—there's obviously something wrong with what *I'm* doing, if nobody else feels this way."

I wonder, is it about the definition of guilt—or the interpretation of what it means in the context of working motherhood?

Perhaps for some, guilt is equated with wrongdoing. So an
admission of guilt is an admission of wrongdoing. The implication being, if a mother feels guilty, she is by definition in
the wrong—she shouldn't be going out to work; she is committing a parenting crime against her children by doing so. If
that's the association, then I can understand why some are denying any feelings of guilt.

But guilt in this context *doesn't* mean wrongdoing. It's just
a by-product of motherhood. We feel guilty if a child falls off
a chair while we answer the door or if we accidentally hurt
the toddler while cutting his nails or if we don't bake a home-
made birthday cake. These little moments of guilt don't mean
we've done something wrong. And similarly, feeling guilty
when a child cries as we leave for work doesn't indicate wrongdoing.

Or perhaps the writers equate guilt with unhappiness? It's
down to interpretation, but for me, it's entirely possible to experience occasional working-mother guilt but to be very happy
overall. This is true for almost all of the twenty-five mothers
I've spoken to for this weekly interview series—most of them
experience guilt, and most of them are happy with their jobs.

I'm not saying embrace the guilt; we do need to keep it at
bay—to make sure it doesn't take hold. But claiming it doesn't
exist at all just creates confusion and divisions.

I just needed to work that out. I'm OK again, in my guilty,
happy world.

"Wisty"

Post Script: Since publishing this, I've had some conversations
online about the fact that "Guilt" just isn't the right word
at all. So I'm going with "wisty" which means I'm wistful for
a world where I could somehow have more time with my

kids, but am also happy at work. I'm wisty, not guilty. If you have other suggestions, let me know.

> "In the United States, there is an inexplicable underappreciation for the sacrifices that are made on a daily basis by millions of mothers across the country."

Family-Friendly Policies Can Help Working Mothers

Marques Lang

Marques Lang is a graduate of Lewis & Clark Law School and a financial planner. In the following viewpoint, he argues that women earn less than men because women are disproportionately required to devote time to child care duties. He says that the federal Family and Medical Leave Act (FMLA) needs to be revised so that women can take time off when a child is born without damaging their career prospects. He also suggests mandating a shorter workweek; this would make it easier for women to balance family responsibilities and remove barriers to their advancement in the workplace.

As you read, consider the following questions:

1. What is the motherhood penalty, according to Lang?

Marques Lang, "Income Disparity for Working Mothers: Eliminating Structural Discrimination Through Public Policy," *PSU McNair Scholars Online Journal*, 2011. © 2011 PSU McNair Scholars Online Journal. Reproduced by permission.

2. What mothers does Lang say are not covered by the FMLA, and why?

3. What does Lang suggest the government could do to encourage employers to provide paid family leave?

Several studies have shown that in the United States mothers earn lower incomes than employees of similar qualifications and productivity levels. This phenomenon is known as the *motherhood penalty*. This [viewpoint] analyzes the antecedents of the motherhood penalty as well as other factors that result in mothers earning lower wages than other women and men, particularly fathers. This begs the question: What role do institutions play in maintaining wage inequality through public policies, specifically maternity leave policy? In answering this question, both the Pregnancy Discrimination Act of 1978 and the Family and Medical Leave Act of 1993 are examined to identify the gaps between current policy and what is needed to promote equality between mothers and non-mothers.

The Motherhood Penalty

Many young girls dream of having a family and children of their own once they grow up; however, in the United States this decision may come with several unintended consequences. Mothers in this country are being put into positions that may force them into choosing between their careers, their individual health, and the betterment of their family dynamic, which has the potential to lead to lose-lose situations. When a mother opts to reduce her workload in order to focus her efforts on raising a family, she is met with various trade-offs that can hinder her ability to be viewed as a productive worker. If the decision is made to shift to part-time work, engage in a flexible schedule, or exit the labor market, the opportunity cost that is associated with such a decision can have a negative effect on a mother's economic status within society due to the financial stability that will be sacrificed in order to raise a family.

This lack of economic stability leads to several other problems as well. First, decreased income leads to higher rates of long-term poverty among mothers. This is due to the fact that lower incomes beget diminished contributions to retirement plans and Social Security, which ultimately leads to smaller income streams for women as they age. Second, children suffer as a result of less time spent with parents, poorer quality of child care received, or the psychological effects associated with not fitting in with peers who have more financially secure parents. Lastly, to put it bluntly, it simply is not fair for parental status to have any influence on a woman's wages.

Once a woman bears children, she can expect to earn less than males and women without children, regardless of the qualification and productivity levels of the individual worker. This phenomenon is known as the *motherhood penalty*. Although the extent of the penalty varies, a number of studies that analyzed U.S. National Longitudinal Survey data between 1968–1998 found that there is a motherhood penalty of 4–7% for one child and an 11–15% for two or more children. This penalty remains present even after accounting for similarities in qualifications such as workforce experience and education, as well as organizational commitment and productivity levels.

Who Is Affected by the Motherhood Penalty?

The motherhood penalty is an element of the wage differential between women and men that specifically refers to mothers earning less than people who are similar in all other respects, in terms of education, occupation, and previous time in the labor force. Literature shows that mothers who are highly educated, experienced and/or married are subjected to a larger motherhood penalty than mothers who do not share these same statuses. A woman with a college education and substantial work experience will typically earn a higher salary than someone with only a high school diploma; therefore, women who reach this status have more to lose post-childbearing. Conversely, women whose human capital factors are less significant typically earn less, thus a smaller penalty is incurred.

Marital status also plays a significant role due to the perceived increase in family commitments. When a partner is present to share the financial responsibilities, it is more feasible for a parent to stay at home with their small children. Consequently, mothers may have more time available to dedicate to their family as opposed to spending this time trying to advance one's career. On the other hand, unmarried mothers are usually more self-supporting, which makes it more likely that they will dedicate more time to career advancement than married mothers, although it should be noted that increased effort by single mothers does not necessarily lead to higher earnings due to the aforementioned motherhood penalties. Furthermore, married men are more likely to have increased job commitment, due to the increase in responsibility that a wife and children carries. This commitment ultimately leads to increased earnings as a result of newfound pay expectations, given that pay expectations typically grant individuals with higher actualized incomes. In addition, some employers may carry beliefs that married men with children both need and deserve higher incomes.

When men become fathers, there is a tendency for their wages to increase. This is known as the fatherhood premium. The premium occurs as a result of the perception that fathers are more able to successfully manage work and family, while becoming more productive and committed to the workplace post-fatherhood. This is due to the fact that employers offer fathers larger salaries as a result of the mentality that men are to serve as breadwinners for the family. . . .

Policies to Help Working Mothers

At the public policy level, the United States is in a very unique position in terms of providing adequate benefits to parents. While there are numerous ways to go about enhancing policies to be more family friendly, the focus of this [viewpoint] will be on leave policies. The two statutes, in the United States, that have had the largest impact on parental leave are the Pregnancy Discrimination Act of 1978 and the Family and Medical Leave Act of 1993. These statutes will be examined to identify the gaps between current policy and what is needed to promote equality between mothers and non-mothers.

The Pregnancy Discrimination Act (PDA) amended Title VII of the Civil Rights Act of 1964. This amendment made it illegal for employers to discriminate against women on the basis of pregnancy, childbirth, or any other related medical condition. Organizations with 15 or more employees are required to abide by this statute. In addition, employers cannot use pregnancy as a basis for hiring and firing decisions, denying leave and health insurance, or in the limiting of fringe benefits that are available to employees who are not pregnant. Essentially, employees who are or become pregnant are treated the same as temporarily disabled employees, and the inequitable treatment of such employees is considered a form of sexual discrimination.

In 1993 the Family and Medical Leave Act (FMLA) was signed into law. The purpose of this law is to provide leave time for employees in order to care for a newborn or adopted child, an elderly parent, or any other family-related issue that may arise. This law affects organizations with 50 or more employees. In order for an employee to be eligible for benefits under FMLA, he must have worked at least 1,250 hours in the preceding 12 months with their current organization. If both of these criteria are met, then the employee is eligible for up to 12 weeks of unpaid leave per year.

Problems with the FMLA

Although both of these statutes provided a boost in the efforts to promote parental equality in the workplace, there is still a large margin for improvement, especially within the FMLA. Based on the eligibility criteria stated above, only 45% of U.S. women qualify for this leave. In 2000, only 16% of those covered by the FMLA used leave, 90% of which did not exercise their rights to use the full 12 weeks due to a lack of pay while on leave. Furthermore, since the Family and Medical Leave Act is only mandatory for businesses with 50 or more employees, there is a portion of the workforce, entrepreneurs and other small business workers, that remain uncovered by the law, which may subject employees to continued abuses that perpetuate the income gap amongst mothers. Lastly, there are a number of employers who do not comply with the law, thus further continuing this cycle of wage disparity.

The FMLA also has a number of other limitations. First, the act focuses on traditional families. It does not provide shelters for single parent households, who require an income in order to survive. And until 2010, domestic partnerships were also excluded. Second, a third of all employers that are affected by the law were already providing benefits that were equal to or greater than the benefits described in the statute. Lastly, in order to be eligible, an employee must have worked 1,250 hours in the preceding 12 months with their current company; however, since many of the lower-paid workers typically have either less than one year of experience, work part time or intermittently, or are individuals who have taken leave, they are not eligible for benefits under the FMLA.

Proposed Changes

A number of analysts have proposed various changes that could potentially aid in reducing the income gap. The most prominent proposals fall into three categories: regulating the workweek, providing benefits to part-time employees, and mandating paid leave.

Regulating the workweek can take shape in a couple of different ways. First, policy could create a standardized workweek that would make full time equivalent to 35 hours a week, without any fear of reprisal such as lack of raises, promotions, or bonuses. This would provide individuals with more family and leisure time, which could lead to a more productive workforce, while potentially helping to redistribute household labor among genders to more equitable levels. However, this would require changes to the Fair Labor Standards Act. For example, overtime laws would need to be adjusted to start at time worked over 35 hours rather than 40 hours. In addition, exemption criteria would have to be reevaluated in order to provide those in management positions the same treatment as subordinate workers. This would also aid in eliminating the glass ceiling that mothers face as a result of not being able to comply with the demanding work schedules that are expected from mid- to upper-level managers. Another, and perhaps more feasible, change would be to allow flexible scheduling in terms of days and hours worked as well as start and finish times. Although the impact of this change would be minimal, it could allow for more family time in the mornings and evenings.

Second, since a number of parents, primarily mothers, work on a part-time basis, due to the family-friendly nature of these jobs, benefits could be given to part-time employees. These benefits could include retirement as well as medical insurance and leave benefits at the same cost to the part-time employee as to full-time employees. It is not uncommon for part-time employees to have to incur larger portions of their insurance premiums, if any are even offered, while earning a smaller wage. Providing these benefits at an affordable rate would have a considerable impact on workforce equality. Also, retirement benefits would go a long way to narrowing the long-term income gap. Mothers who either work part time or opt to leave the labor market also lose their retirement contributions. This leads to mothers' continued social and economic struggle not only during peak childbearing years but in the golden years as well.

Failing at Family-Friendly Policies

Lastly, mandating paid leave could perhaps have the most significant impact on a parent's ability to adequately care for a child. However, this would require a great deal of compromise between policy makers and organizations. One such way to appease both sides could be to offer a tax incentive to organizations that provide paid leave. This would allow organizations to continue to maintain their bottom line, while providing parents with the income that they require. The reduction in national tax revenue could be made up by the increased number of individuals who remain in the workforce who otherwise would have dropped out. The more people there are in the labor market, the more taxpayers there are in the pool, which is beneficial to all the parties involved.

Policy reform will be of the utmost importance when it comes to remedying pay discrimination against mothers. Of all the industrialized countries in the world, the United States is among the worst when it comes to instituting family-friendly parental leave policies. This must change if there is to be pay equality, since there is a strong association between good leave policies and mothers' capacity to reenter and remain active participants in the workforce post-childbearing. Furthermore, it has been shown that good policies increase workforce attachment among women, for it allows mothers to better balance work and family life without taking extended withdrawals from the market. These types of policies may allow mothers to feel as if their contribution to the workplace is valued, in addition to allowing their relationships with the organization and its members to be nurtured. Ultimately, this increase in experience, rather than extended

An Overview of the FMLA

The FMLA [Family and Medical Leave Act] entitles eligible employees of covered employers to take unpaid, job-protected leave for specified family and medical reasons with continuation of group health insurance coverage under the same terms and conditions as if the employee had not taken leave. Eligible employees are entitled to:

Twelve workweeks of leave in a 12-month period for:

- the birth of a child and to care for the newborn child within one year of birth;
- the placement with the employee of a child for adoption or foster care and to care for the newly placed child within one year of placement;
- to care for the employee's spouse, child, or parent who has a serious health condition;
- a serious health condition that makes the employee unable to perform the essential functions of his or her job;
- any qualifying exigency arising out of the fact that the employee's spouse, son, daughter, or parent is a covered military member on "covered active duty;" or

Twenty-six workweeks of leave during a single 12-month period to care for a covered service member with a serious injury or illness if the eligible employee is the service member's spouse, son, daughter, parent, or next of kin (military caregiver leave).

United States Department of Labor,
"Family and Medical Leave Act," 2014.

leave from or exiting the market, will provide mothers with higher salaries, thus helping to close the wage gap.

More Needs to Be Done

It goes without stating that mothers play an invaluable role in the development of societies throughout the world. However, in the United States there is an inexplicable underappreciation for the sacrifices that are made on a daily basis by millions of mothers across the country. Mothers are being relegated to traditional gender roles in the home and are experiencing a glass ceiling in the workplace. If wages are truly determined by a "free" market system, one can conclude that the contributions of mothers in this market are perceived to be less valuable than those of fathers, which is contributing to large wage disparities among genders in the labor market. Despite the increases in the number of women who are college educated, they only reap rewards similar to men when they opt to not have children and maintain a continuous presence in the labor market; however, this alternative too often comes at the expense of one's potential family life. Therefore, a choice that many women must consider is one of family and children, career with minimal family interaction, or the career as a stand-alone.

With that being said, there has been progress made in the past two decades when it comes to women as mothers and workers. In the mid-1980s, it was estimated that women spent approximately 9 years out of the labor market. In 2000, this gap narrowed to 4.6 years. There are several factors that could explain this shift, such as falling real male wages, favorable public and corporate policies, more opportunities for part-time employment, and men sharing more of the household duties.

However, in order to continue to take strides toward greater gender equality in the labor market, while ensuring more work-life balance, a paradigmatic shift in societal thinking must occur. As a society, we must begin to realize that the gender income gap is not just a woman or mother problem, but it is a family and cultural issue that affects everyone. The current system has not worked because most families simply cannot afford to take unpaid leave without falling into economic hardship. Therefore, in many instances it is not a *choice* for mothers to accept lower paying jobs rather it is an obligation in an attempt to make ends meet. In order for progress to be made, it will be vital for our society to start enacting the family values that we so frequently espouse to ensure the facilitation of tangible change in our communities moving forward.

> *"Plenty of evidence suggests it's not the act of having children that hurts women's careers, but the family-friendly workplace policies ostensibly designed to support new parents."*

Is Maternity Leave a Bad Idea?

Tamsin McMahon

Tamsin McMahon is an associate editor at Maclean's, *where she covers business and the economy. In the following viewpoint, she argues that Canada's yearlong paid maternity leave may hurt women. McMahon says that women who take a long time away from work have trouble returning to the workforce and have lower career earnings over their lifetimes. She suggests that both men and women should be encouraged to find ways to balance work and family, including working part time or staying connected to the office while on maternity (or paternity) leave.*

As you read, consider the following questions:

1. According to McMahon, how much can a 3 percent wage penalty a year cost a woman over her lifetime?

2. What is the "maternity buddy" program launched by public relations firm Edelman?

Tamsin McMahon, "Is Maternity Leave a Bad Idea?," *Maclean's*, January 20, 2014. © 2014 Maclean's. Reproduced by permission.

3. What workplace policies has Quebec instituted specifically for fathers, and what benefits does McMahon say
this may have?

Shortly after Julia announced to the partners at her Toronto-
area law firm that she was pregnant, she found herself being given less work to do. And the company immediately began interviewing for her replacement as head of the firm's
human rights and employment law department. "I became a
ghost in the building," she says. "They told me in a meeting,
'We don't know, you could go into labour at any moment.' At
three months pregnant. I was like, 'Really?'"

When she found herself being cut out of workplace emails
after her maternity leave started last March, she began to as-
sess her options: come back to work after a year and struggle
to be taken seriously, or use the time off to start her own legal
business. With her daughter in tow, she began combing
through her network of contacts and meeting for coffee with
prospective clients, including some she recruited through a
mom's group she organized. With two months left on her maternity leave, Julia has plans to hire a babysitter once a week
so she can get her business up and running in time to tell her
firm she's leaving.

For Julia (not her real name), 38, the treatment she received after she announced she was pregnant came as both a
shock and confirmation of the message she had heard repeatedly in her career at some of Canada's biggest law firms: "We
would go out for drinks, the ties would come off and the men
would say: 'I see a wedding band on a man and I think, 'Amazing, because that guy's got to pay the bills and make sure the
woman and children are happy,'" she says. "'When I see a
wedding band on a woman, the first thing I think is liability,
because I know that 90 per cent of the time I'm going to have
to deal with a pregnancy.'"

Her experience echoes what researchers have long
chronicled: Pregnancy is among the greatest roadblocks to

women's professional success. But while the debate is often framed as a tug-of-war between women's career ambitions and their desire to be involved mothers, plenty of evidence suggests it's not the act of having children that hurts women's careers, but the family-friendly workplace policies ostensibly designed to support new parents. In particular, the yearlong maternity leave that has become one of the most prized benefits offered to working mothers in Canada.

When the federal government doubled the unemployment benefits offered to parents more than a decade ago, it was hailed as one of the most important public policy advancements aimed both at helping workers navigate the transition into parenthood and ensuring enough of the all-important time for new infants to bond with their parents. While the government was careful to allow moms and dads the right to split the 37-week "parental leave" portion of its yearlong benefit program, that quickly morphed into a full year away from work for mothers, often followed a year or two later by another yearlong leave for a second child. Nearly 90 per cent of new mothers took a parental leave, averaging 48 weeks, according to a 2009 Statistics Canada study. By comparison, just 11 per cent of men outside of Quebec, which has its own paternity leave program, took any paid time off work, averaging just 2.4 weeks.

Few in Canada would argue that paid, job-protected parental leave is a bad thing for families, although the U.K. government quietly considered scrapping the country's yearlong maternity-leave program in 2011 as a way to boost economic growth. At the time, the female head of a right-wing think tank that championed the proposal argued that maternity benefits "too often lead to a downward spiral of earnings and career, a life of near-dependence on the state . . . and probably an impoverished old age."

That's an extreme view and there is ample evidence that countries without any paid parental-leave benefits suffer from having fewer women in the workforce. But the debate over maternity leave raises a number of uncomfortable questions: Could a full year off be too long? Are parents shooting themselves in the foot when they use their hard-won benefits as an opportunity to completely shut themselves off from work?

In practice, the workplace gender imbalances that maternity leave has encouraged hold profound implications for women's long-term earnings and career advancement. In a 2010 study examining why women continue to earn 20 per cent less over the course of their careers than their male colleagues, TD Economics found that as much as half of the wage gap was due to women taking time off work to raise children. Women lost three per cent of their earnings for each year they were away from work, a penalty that persisted long after they went back to their jobs. While meant as a one-year break, parental leaves also have a way of stretching beyond a year, with some women opting to follow up their paid leave with an unpaid career break of a month or even years, putting them even further behind. A penalty of three per cent a year might sound like a small price to pay for that time off, but the study's authors estimated a woman who works for six years at a $64,000-a-year job, takes three years off to raise kids and then goes back to work full time for another 20 years, would lose $325,000 over the course of her career. That includes the money she received from collecting unemployment benefits on maternity leave.

What's more, they found that the wage penalty was three times greater for women who had taken multiple short absences from work—jumping in and out of the workplace to have more than one child—than those who took a single long break, even if it amounted to the same total time away from work. Employers, they said, tended to view multiple absences as a sign that female employees aren't committed to their job. That pay gap between men and women also has implications for the broader economy. A 2009 report from the University of Canberra estimated that closing Australia's 17 per cent gender pay gap would add roughly $90 billion to the country's economy.

The consequences of women taking a year from work are often far greater than money. A study last year by Cornell University economists Francine Blau and Lawrence Kahn compared the careers of women in the U.S., where federal laws allow for just 12 weeks of unpaid parental leave, to Western countries, including Canada, that had long paid leave benefits for parents. They found that while women were more likely to drop out of the workforce in the U.S., those who kept working were far more likely to be in high-paying jobs, senior management and traditionally male careers like science and engineering. America's most famous female tech executives, Sheryl Sandberg and Marissa Mayer, both admitted they took almost no break from work after giving birth. Equal numbers of men and women work as managers in the U.S., while in countries with long, paid maternity leaves, half as many women are in management as men. Many women in those countries also end up in low-paying and part-time jobs. In Canada, two-thirds of part-time workers are women, a number that hasn't budged in 30 years. In short, family-friendly policies such as maternity leave may encourage women to settle for lower-paying jobs, the Cornell economists concluded, while in a perverse twist America's sink-or-swim workplace culture has encouraged more women to stick it out on the career ladder. The so-called motherhood penalty at work may be well established, but researchers say the underlying assumption that women are simply choosing to scale back because of a desire to spend more time with their children is deeply flawed. "The issue has been framed in some media outlets that women are basically answering the call of motherhood and wanting to be there for their children and are dropping out," says Souha Ezzedeen, a professor of human resource management at York University, who studies gender issues in the workplace. "On the other hand, sound scholarly research suggests that they're pushed out because of the level of inflexibility in the workplace, especially when you're moving up the ranks."

Last year, Florida State University professor Irene Padavic and Harvard Business School professor Robin Ely published a paper recounting their experience being hired by a large professional service firm to find out why so many of its female employees were leaving. After interviewing 100 employees, they found that both men and women complained about the punishing 65-hour workweeks. The turnover rate, they found, was actually the same for both men and women, with men equally as likely to complain about work-life balance as women. The only real difference between the sexes was that female employees were far more likely to take advantage of some of the firm's family-friendly policies, including maternity leave—policies supposedly designed to protect their careers, but which ultimately got them crossed off the list for promotions.

Management later rejected their conclusions, they said, because their recommendations weren't focused exclusively on women. The belief "that gender was the firm's primary HR problem, that the nature of the gender problem was women's difficulty balancing work and family, and that men were largely immune to such difficulties," wasn't backed up by evidence, they wrote. Instead, the notion that women, but not men, have a biological imperative to spend less time at work had become a convenient "diversion" that allowed the company to ignore larger problems in its corporate culture. Indeed, there is a growing body of research suggesting men may face an even greater career backlash from staying home with children than women do, which may be one reason why so few opt to take a leave. In an issue devoted to the topic published last June, the U.S. *Journal of Social Issues* found that men who asked for flexible working arrangements were more likely to be laid off, while those who had taken time off work for family reasons earned 26.4 per cent less in the long term compared to those who hadn't—a larger penalty than the 23.2 per cent drop in earnings for women. The research suggests it's the leave, and not the gender of the person taking it, that is the problem.

Some companies have started creating programs to encourage new mothers to stay connected with the office. The Toronto office of global PR firm Edelman launched a "maternity buddy" program in 2010 that pairs female employees on leave with a female coworker to meet for coffee or lunch and chat about new hires, big projects or office gossip. "We're in an industry that has dramatically changed over the last several years," says general manager Lisa Kimmel. "People were really struggling, not only to make that transition in terms of balancing all the new personal responsibilities, but also in terms of making sure the skills to do their job effectively were also polished and up-to-date, given that a lot changes in a year."

Last year alone, 15 of the company's 130 employees participated in the program. No one has quit and the bulk of the participants have since been promoted. Kimmel herself was a buddy to an employee who arranged to be involved with a particularly important new project that started after she went on maternity leave. Despite the program's success, Kimmel says the company may launch a formal on-boarding program for returning mothers, similar to what they give to new hires, since many women feel overwhelmed by the sheer amount of change that happened while they were gone. "Some people said, 'I felt like I was starting a new job,'" she says.

Still, the pressure in Canada for women to shut themselves off completely from work for a year after the birth of a child can be intense. After finding herself bored and lonely during a four-month maternity leave for her first son, Reva Seth, a former corporate lawyer turned consultant and author, opted to take just two weeks for her second son. "I got really horrible responses a lot of times from people about why I wasn't with my baby all the time after two weeks," she says, even though as a self-employed consultant she wasn't eligible for maternity-leave benefits at the time. Her experiences inspired Seth to write *The MomShift*, a book based on 500 interviews with women whose careers took off after having children, due to be published next month by Random House Canada.

The concept of a year away from work to care for a new baby was fine in a time when most workers could expect to spend their entire careers at the same company, often in the same job, she says. But fundamental changes to the Canadian economy are encouraging more women to become their family's primary breadwinner and forcing more workers, both men and women, into self-employment and temporary contract jobs.

Seth argues those trends are rewriting the rules when it comes to maternity leave. While changes to federal employment laws in 2011 now allow self-employed workers to claim parental leave benefits, few of today's female entrepreneurs can afford to quit working for a year and let their professional network lapse. "The way we view motherhood is changing, underwritten by the seismic shift in how our careers are going to change completely," she says.

The notion of combining work and maternity leave is gaining traction among many of today's mothers who say that completely cutting themselves off from work for a year would be devastating to their career advancement. Weeks after Kristin Taylor made partner at her Bay Street law firm in 2001, she found out she was pregnant. Having spent her entire career in corporate law, Taylor had watched other women at the firm return from long maternity leaves and struggle to adjust to the breakneck pace of change at the office. So before she went on leave, Taylor divided her clients into three groups: those she could delegate to coworkers, those important enough to have her home number in case of emergencies, and those

Taylor judged so crucial to her success at the firm she actively worked for them while on leave. For Taylor, who didn't receive unemployment benefits but continued to collect her salary from the firm while on leave, that meant spending an hour or two a day on the computer at nap time and taking calls while breastfeeding or at Gymboree classes. "I found it helpful to use my brain in a different way," says Taylor, now a partner at Cassels Brock. "There were a couple of days when if I read, 'Moo, baa and lalala' another time I was going to lose my mind."

It also made for a smooth transition when Taylor opted to return to work after five months on a modified four-day schedule. She found the strategy so successful that she repeated it two years later when she gave birth to her second daughter, opting to take on even more professional responsibilities during her seven-month leave. She says both employers and employees need to have realistic expectations when it comes to how much involvement new mothers should have with their jobs after giving birth, so that maternity leave doesn't become disruptive to either the company or women's careers. "It's ultimately really how you want your life to look, how you want parenting to look," says Taylor, who is an employment lawyer. "But we get really hung up in a way that's not always constructive about the sacred cow that maternity leave is. When, really, what we should be thinking of is the long-term career progression and how to balance that along the way."

Critics point out that work-life balance policies such as parental leave are typically aimed exclusively at women and that if more men were encouraged to take time off work to care for infants, then women's careers wouldn't suffer as much. By introducing policies aimed specifically at fathers, such as Quebec's five weeks of paid paternity leave exclusively for fathers, advocates say both governments and employers can make becoming a working parent less of a gender issue. "To the extent that workplaces get used to men, too, taking leave, that can only be a good thing in terms of gender equity at work and at home," says University of Calgary sociologist Gillian Ranson, who has studied nontraditional families, including stay-at-home fathers and same-sex parents.

A federal government pilot project launched in 2012 that allows people to keep more of their unemployment benefits— including parental leave—if they earn money from work should also give women more flexibility to combine career and maternity leave and encourage more employers to reach out to new mothers during their time off. Even without any new HR programs or policy interventions, the growing number of women who are their family's primary breadwinner means more couples may simply decide to split their leave benefits differently out of economic necessity.

For Julia, being cut out of the workplace loop while on maternity leave ended up becoming a blessing in disguise since it convinced her that her career would be better off in the long run if she tried to strike it out on her own. "If I were coming back, I'd be pretty hurt and disenfranchised. But I don't feel that residual guilt that I would if they were treating me well and trying to get me to come to this barbecue or that client event," she says. "So far, it's just been empowering."

Periodical and Internet Sources Bibliography

The following articles have been selected to supplement the diverse views presented in this chapter.

Rebecca Adams	"Biological Proof That Home Is More Stressful than the Office for Working Moms," *Huffington Post*, July 17, 2014.
Gina Bellafante	"Sympathy for the Working Mother," *New York Times*, May 23, 2014.
Jillian Berman	"The Working Mom Problem No One Is Talking About," *Huffington Post*, February 14, 2014.
Stephanie Coontz	"The Triumph of the Working Mother," *New York Times*, June 1, 2013.
Bryce Covert	"No, Working Moms Are Not Ruining Their Children," *ThinkProgress*, June 23, 2014.
Petula Dvorak	"Welcome to Overwhelmia: The Modern-Day Madness of Working Mothers," *Washington Post*, March 13, 2014.
Maggie Fox	"Working Moms May Be Helping Their Kids, Study Finds," NBC News, June 16, 2014.
Tovah Klein	"Working Mothers, Raising Children: Something's Gotta Give," *Psychology Today*, March 18, 2014.
Belinda Luscombe	"What Our Culture of Overwork Is Doing to Mothers," *Time*, July 30, 2014.
Margie Warrell	"Letter to Working Mothers: Stop Feeling So Guilty," *Forbes*, June 25, 2013.
Claire Zulkey	"Why I Stopped Apologizing for Being a Working Mother," *Fast Company*, August 18, 2014.

CHAPTER 3

Does the Lean-In Movement Help Working Women?

Chapter Preface

Sheryl Sandberg is the chief operating officer (COO) at Facebook, making her one of the most powerful people in the technology industry. In 2013 she published *Lean In: Women, Work, and the Will to Lead*, in which she encourages women to commit to high-powered careers, ask for salary increases, and "lean in" to their careers. The book sparked much controversy and discussion about the roles of careers in women's lives and ongoing gender discrimination in the workplace and in society at large.

In 2014 Sandberg inaugurated another related campaign, titled "Ban Bossy." Along with Anna Maria Chávez, chief executive officer (CEO) of Girl Scouts of the United States of America, Sandberg wrote an op-ed in the *Wall Street Journal* in which she and Chávez posit that the term "bossy" is used to try to stifle girls' ambition and leadership. Sandberg and Chávez explain,

> The word "bossy" has carried both a negative and a female connotation for more than a century. The first citation of "bossy" in the Oxford English Dictionary refers to an 1882 article in *Harper's Magazine*, which declared: "There was a lady manager who was dreadfully bossy." A Google Ngram analysis of digitized books over the past 100 years found that the use of "bossy" to describe women first peaked in the Depression-era 1930s, when popular sentiment held that a woman should not "steal" a job from a man, and reached its highest point in the mid-1970s as the women's movement ramped up and more women entered the workforce.

Some commenters feel that Sandberg and Chávez's campaign is misguided. Cathy Young writing at RealClearPolitics argues that there is little evidence that the word "bossy" does real harm to girls, pointing out that in a large 2008 study "girls and boys were equally likely to say they wanted to be leaders." Robin Abcarian of the *Los Angeles Times* argues that "calling someone 'bossy' is barely an insult. It is not the same as calling someone a fascist or a dictator, or even a control freak." Alice Robb in the *New Statesman*, on the other hand, argues that studies have shown that "bossy" is a term applied disproportionately to women. She quotes Lynne Murphy, a linguist at the University of Sussex, who explains that "people say things like 'lady boss' or 'woman boss' but not 'man boss'— because 'boss' is already stereotyped as male. 'Bossy' as applied to women and girls gives the impression that they somehow don't have the right to be the boss, that they are acting in a socially inappropriate or unacceptable way."

The following chapter explores other controversies sur-rounding Sandberg's social initiatives and considers whether leaning in to careers helps or harms working women.

> "We have to celebrate every positive moment. . . . But I want to say, 'Thank you, but not enough. We want more. We want real equality.'"

Leaning In Can Help Women Achieve Career Success

Sheryl Sandberg, as told to Cindi Leive

Sheryl Sandberg is the chief operating officer of Facebook, an activist, and the author of Lean In: Women, Work, and the Will to Lead. *Cindi Leive is the editor in chief of* Glamour *magazine. In the following viewpoint, Sandberg talks about how women can be successful in their careers. She encourages women to negotiate for salary increases, to ask men to help with child care duties, and not to be afraid to commit to work. Sandberg says that it is possible to balance a family and a career, and she asks both men and women to work toward equality.*

As you read, consider the following questions:

1. According to Sandberg, what inequities remain in women's wages?

2. What evidence does Sandberg say demonstrates that it is possible for women to work and have a family?

3. What does Sandberg mean when she says "don't leave before you leave"?

Just 12 months ago, Sheryl Sandberg was a Silicon Valley tech executive—a rising star who'd begun her career in Washington, D.C., before skyrocketing to the top of Google and leapfrogging to Facebook as Mark Zuckerberg's right hand.

Then came *Lean In[: Women, Work, and the Will to Lead]*.

Sandberg's blockbuster career manifesto—arguing that women hold themselves back from pursuing their careers but should instead "sit at the table," literally and figuratively, alongside their male colleagues—sparked a raging global debate about work, women, and motherhood. Sandberg, 44, a mother of two, instantly became both a lightning rod for critics (one charged she was "blaming other women for not trying hard enough") and a 360-degree life guru for millions of women worldwide, who went on to found thousands of Lean In Circles to help one another reach their own job goals. The column you're reading is a new one for *Glamour*, dedicated to career advice from women in all kinds of top jobs. Who better to start with than the woman who kicked off our current national conversation? When I met her at Facebook's headquarters, in Menlo Park, California, she was fresh off a plane from Washington, D.C., and highly focused, even though [Facebook chief executive officer (CEO)] Mark Zuckerberg was chatting with colleagues (hoodie-less, if you're curious) just outside our glass-walled conference room. Here, some highlights from our conversation.

The Book

CINDI LEIVE: Let's start with the book. Lean In *has sold more than 1.5 million copies. There are over 12,000 Lean In Circles in 50 countries. The phrase* lean in *itself has become a meme! Did you expect this?*

SHERYL SANDBERG: I had no idea. I wrote the book hoping we would have a big conversation on gender—but what I've been most excited about is that people have really started to change their lives.

CL: So you're seeing young women's behavior shift? Are they sitting at the table?

SS: Well, when *I'm* in the room! [*Laughs.*] But yes ... and the other thing that's changed is that everywhere I go, women tell me they're getting raises—and CEOs tell me I have cost them so much money. [*Laughs.*]

CL: Well, that's a victory! Since Lean In *came out, there have been a lot of high-profile appointments of women: Janet Yellen, the first female chair of the Federal Reserve; Mary Barra, the first female CEO of General Motors [Company]; Marjorie Scardino on the board of Twitter. Those are significant moments, aren't they?*

SS: We have to celebrate every positive moment.... But I want to say, "Thank you, but not enough. We want more. We want real equality." Progress is still very slow. The numbers [of women leaders] are still really, really low. We just had two female heads of state elected. That brings the total to about 18.

More Progress Is Needed

CL: That's a record, by the way.

SS: But it's not a lot; there are slightly under 200 countries in the world! After the November 2012 elections [which saw the number of women in the Senate rise to 20], people were writing that women were taking over the Senate. Twenty seats out of 100 is not a takeover! There's been no progress in women's wages—particularly women of color—over the past 10 years. The average woman makes 77 cents compared with the average man; it's 64 cents for African Americans and 54 cents for Latinas. Those numbers have not moved since 2002. And people say things to me every day showing a lack of understanding of the situation.

CL: *What kinds of things?*

SS: "It's not an issue in *my* industry." "It's better in *my* industry." Actually, it's not that good in any industry! Or people say, "She's too aggressive" [about a woman employee, but not a man]. It happens all the time. Now, at least, people are seeing the problem. [Cisco CEO] John Chambers invited me to a senior-management meeting of his top 400 people. He stood there on the stage and said, "I thought we were doing this well, and we're not. Every single senior woman in this company, we called all of you too aggressive. We're sorry, and we're not going to do it anymore." From a CEO, that's amazing.

CL: *Wow.*

SS: [And recently] I was in Beijing, meeting the first Lean In Circle there. The 13 women in it were mostly what's known there as "leftover" women: over 27 and unmarried. They talked about making their own choices, pursuing careers. I started crying because it was my dream, seeing women like that talk about their empowerment. I've been to Circles of military women in Minneapolis and of college women in D.C. One Circle told me every person there made a major change—their husbands help at home, or they got promoted.

I'm excited that more people, especially men, are understanding that equality is good for them. I don't want men to want equality for women because they're being nice to their colleagues and daughters. I want men to want it because it's better for their companies and their lives.

CL: *We actually did a survey last year of* Glamour *readers and found that about 20 percent* fewer *women today than in the seventies wanted their boss's job.*

SS: That's very in keeping with the research I've seen.

Job and Family

CL: *Well, at Facebook, you're* that woman younger women look at and draw conclusions about. What do you want them to know about having the big job *and* a family at the same time?

SS: I want them to know it's possible. It's not easy, though it's certainly easier for me than for a lot of people. I guess I also want them to know it's fulfilling: I want them to have "and" language rather than "or" language. Men feel like they can be a professional *and* a father. For women it's "or." That's offensive to me because 70 percent of mothers in this country work full time. They have to! So this concept that it's not possible is crazy. . . . [Even in Hollywood] I can't name a show or movie where the female lead character works and has kids and isn't frazzled. I can't think of any who work and are *happy*.

CL: Most of the best female characters on TV right now are actually single, no kids.

SS: Well, that's another issue—it's sending the message that you can't have [kids and a career].

CL: Let's talk about negotiation. You think women leave money on the table.

SS: Yes. Most women who have not gotten raises have also not asked. If women negotiated their first salary, they'd earn up to an extra $500,000 by the time they were 60.

CL: You tell women to start that negotiation by saying, "I know women don't always get paid as much as men." But is that productive?

SS: That's one option. Both men and women react negatively when women negotiate on their own behalf. Now, a man can just negotiate: "I have a better offer. That's not enough to make my family's ends meet." No one feels bad about it. But when a woman does that, there's a backlash. How do you get out of the backlash? You have to make it not only about you. You can explain that negotiating skills are something you bring to the table—that's what I did with Mark [Zuckerberg]; I said, "You realize you're hiring me to run our deal teams, so you want me to be good at this." Or you can ground it in an outside fact that is tied to the com-

"I'd love to play house, Kevin, but I've got a business to run."

© Marty Bucella/ Cartoonstock.

munity—"I know women are paid less, and I'm concerned about that." Now women are grounding [requests for a raise] in the book!

CL: As in, "Sheryl Sandberg told me to"?

SS: People say, "I read *Lean In*, and I'd like to negotiate." I never thought to suggest it!

Criticism of *Lean In*

CL: I want to talk about some of the criticism of the book. There seemed to be two camps of critics: first, the patently ridiculous, like one columnist calling you "women's worst enemy," which I suppose would make you worse than the Taliban.

SS: I knew there would be people who did not agree with me. This is personal stuff; I'm talking about who we are as parents, as mothers, as fathers.

CL: But then there were more sane arguments that Lean In *was only half the picture, that no amount of women leaning in helps if there are structural policies in place, like you don't get a paid maternity leave. Is that reasonable?*

SS: I completely agree with that. In the intro to my book, I write that there's a chicken and an egg. I wanted to focus more on one part of it, but one begets the other. Companies that have more women in senior roles have better work-life policies. Of course we *should* have paid maternity leave.

CL: What about better child care?

SS: [*Nods.*] It's a huge issue. Now, I'd like some of these issues to be parent issues, not just women's issues.

CL: I like that you actually make a point of telling women on your team, "If you're thinking of starting a family one day, I'm here to help." How do people react? Is anyone like, "Boss, stop talking about my uterus"?

SS: Certainly people will misinterpret what I say, but I'm very careful. My brother's a pediatric neurosurgeon, and he said to a woman he was interviewing, "You may want to have kids one day. If so, that's none of my business, but I also watched my sisters and wife struggle through this. So my door's open. And I will not give the good surgeries to some guy [just] because you're pregnant." That's how people should do it.

CL: Have you had that conversation with men on your team too?

SS: Probably not as much as I should. I don't see men holding themselves back as much because of this, but you're making a good point.

Men and Leaning In

CL: Let's talk about men in general. You say that women have to make their partners equal partners. How can, say, a 25-year-old woman tell if the guy she's dating will help out? Is it as simple as asking?

SS: Ask! There's a lot that needs to be fixed in dating for men and women in our country—there's a lot of pressure on women to do things they may not want to do. And if you start out unequal, you are not going to end up with equality. I'm not suggesting you discuss diaper duty on a first date. But if it's serious, and you want a career, talk about it.

CL: What mistakes by young women still make you cringe?

SS: The "Don't leave before you leave" stuff is alive and well. [In *Lean In*, Sandberg wrote that women often start curbing their professional ambitions years before they have children, out of fear that a demanding job will make work-life balance difficult.]

CL: But a lot of women just don't want a frenetic schedule. What does it mean for them *to lean in?*

SS: I've never argued for anyone to lean in all the time, or even that you have to be in the workplace. I *am* arguing loudly and unapologetically that six years before you have a child, leaning back is stupid. As you get more senior, you get more control of your schedule. I leave work at 5:30 p.m. There are no meetings with me at 6:00 p.m. I'm gone.

CL: In the book, you wrote about how when you were named to Forbes' *World's 100 Most Powerful Women list in 2011, you were embarrassed. Last year you were on the cover of* Fortune's *50 Most Powerful Women issue. Are you more comfortable with the "most powerful" label now?*

SS: No, I didn't cooperate with that article. I begged them not to do that.

CL: Why? I mean, you are *powerful.*

SS: For all the reasons I wrote about in the book! I'm not writing about things *other* women do. I'm writing for other women to have more self-confidence because I need it myself! And if more women were in power, I would . . . feel more comfortable.

CL: What about money? Much of the criticism of Lean In *mentioned your wealth, the implication being that even though you're self-made, you're not qualified to give career advice ["She's a billionaire," wrote one reporter dismissively]. I can't imagine somebody saying that of Warren Buffett or Bill Gates.*

SS: [*Nods and extends both arms in a "Yep, there you have it" gesture.*]

Future Hopes

CL: What's next in your career? There are many companies where you could be CEO. You've chosen to be here. Why?

SS: I really love what we do. I think Facebook does something really important.

CL: People ask if you'll run for office.

SS: I'm doing all the leaning I can!

CL: Well, they say that women have to be asked seven times before they run.

SS: I've been asked more than seven times, so it hasn't happened yet.

CL: As you've said before, nobody really does it all. What's one thing you're not doing now?

SS: Oh my God. So many things. I do everything badly. I do everything less well than I'd like to do it—

CL: You need to give yourself a break!

SS:—and I miss stuff. Things with my kids. Other mothers volunteer more in class. But it's working out. So far, so good.

CL: Decades from now, what do you want to be remembered for?

SS: I think all of us want the same things. We want to be good to the people around us and for our lives to have meaning. For me, that means making the world a little bit easier for women. Someone told me they went to their child's first-grade parent-teacher conference, and the teacher said, "Last year I would have called your daughter bossy. But I read this book, and I'm going to say she has leadership skills." That's what I want. I want that little girl not to be discouraged, at age six, from leading, but encouraged. And if I can play a role in doing that, that's awesome.

Secrets of the Office Master

Sandberg's top tricks for keeping it all together:

WHAT TIME DO YOU GO TO BED AND WAKE UP?

"I sleep from 10:30 or 11:00 p.m. until 5:30 or 6:00 a.m. I try to get seven hours of sleep every night."

GIVE US YOUR TOP LIFE-ORGANIZING STRATEGY.

"I always have a notebook. I'm such a geek. People think I'm crazy—I'm the only one [at Facebook] with a notebook!"

HOW DO YOU CONTROL EMAIL OVERLOAD?

"My motto is 'Done is better than perfect.' I try to do it quickly. I think people really appreciate fast answers."

BEST EVERYDAY WORK ADVICE?

"Have someone who praises you publicly. It's hard for women to praise themselves, but I can say, 'What Andrea did is amazing!'"

WHAT ARE YOUR RULES FOR MAKING YOUR HOME LIFE SANE?

"We don't have phones at meals. And my husband and I try not to travel at the same time."

> *"The public remains conflicted about the impact working mothers have on their young children, with only 21% of Americans saying it's a good thing."*

The Myth of Balancing Motherhood and a Successful Career

Sarah Hoye

Sarah Hoye is a national correspondent for America Tonight *at Al Jazeera America; she was previously a journalist for CNN. In the following viewpoint, she argues that Sheryl Sandberg's lean-in movement is flawed in its effort to encourage more women to commit to their careers. Hoye says that Sandberg, who is wealthy and successful, does not fully address the barriers faced by women who are not wealthy. Hoye says that there are institutional barriers that make choosing career success more difficult for women, and she suggests that as long as those barriers are in place, women will not be as successful in the workplace, whether they lean in to their careers or not.*

As you read, consider the following questions:

1. According to the viewpoint, why did Maria Kefalas decide to pull back on her career?

2. What three things does Sandberg say women can do to further their careers?

3. What evidence is there that the American public is conflicted about working mothers, according to Hoye?

She's a top corporate executive, she leaves work every day at 5:30 p.m. so she can have dinner with her kids, and now Facebook COO [chief operating officer] Sheryl Sandberg is here to help working moms figure out how to follow her successful model.

Recovering Supermom

Not surprisingly, Sandberg's effort to lead a new feminist movement among working professional mothers—outlined in her new book *Lean In: Women, Work, and the Will to Lead*, and her accompanying online campaign—has triggered a debate:

Is a high-powered executive who earns more than $30 million a year the best person to advise other working moms on how to advance their careers?

Maria Kefalas—a university professor, author and married mother of three—can trace a lot of similarities between her career and Sandberg's, without the multimillion-dollar salary, of course.

Like Sandberg, Kefalas achieved amazing career successes while balancing a busy family life by the time she reached her early 40s.

"My career had been so important to me, so central to my life," said Kefalas, a self-described "recovering supermom." "I wrote three books, was a full professor at 42 and was successful in my field."

Last summer, everything changed. Her husband had just spent a rough year undergoing chemotherapy for cancer when her youngest daughter was diagnosed with a serious illness.

Kefalas, like many other working parents, had a choice to make: go for a big promotion or spend more time with her ailing daughter.

It was a no-brainer, she said.

"In a second, it all evaporated and it was gone," she said, of advancing her career. "And I didn't give a rat's ass."

Today, Kefalas is a sociology professor at Saint Joseph's University in Philadelphia and director of the university's Richard Johnson Center for Anti-Violence. Her schedule allows her to spend her precious time with her family, something she might have given up if she had pursued that promotion.

She said she believes the "dramatic and tragic" story of why she "had to stop moving up the academic ladder" speaks to the real-world obstacles that working mothers face all the time.

That's something that Kefalas said Sandberg's good fortune and financial resources have allowed her to escape.

"All mothers have to make choices and we're judged differently," she said. "The choices for working mothers are more costly than it is for men.

"And until that changes, you'll have women opting out."

'Lean In' or 'Wise Up'?

Sandberg's mission is to help create more female business leaders like herself. She believes women can do that by taking charge of their careers, to "lean in" rather than "pull back" when facing obstacles, she wrote in her book, which will be released on Monday [in March 2013].

"Women rarely make one big decision to leave the workforce. Instead, they make a lot of small decisions along the way," Sandberg wrote, according to a book excerpt on Time-.com. "A law associate might decide not to shoot for partner because someday she hopes to have a family. A sales rep might take a smaller territory or not apply for a management role. A teacher might pass on leading curriculum development for her school.

"Often without even realizing it, women stop reaching for new opportunities."

That, she said, has resulted in what she calls a stalled revolution for all women.

"A truly equal world would be one where women ran half of our countries and companies and men ran half of our homes," she wrote.

She's not just interested in selling books, either. Sandberg's Lean In campaign promises to support women through community, education and small groups by offering "ongoing inspiration and support to help them achieve their goals."

"Women are held back by many things, including bias and lack of opportunity," Sandberg said in her "Welcome to Lean In" video, adding "We also hold ourselves back."

In her book, Sandberg outlined three things women can do to further their careers: don't slow down their career before deciding to start a family, let go of unattainable goals, and make sure their colleagues are aware when women are held to different standards than men, particularly when women succeed.

The book hadn't even hit the shelves before everyone from every corner started weighing in. . . .

Sandberg's push to get women into the corner office and at the conference table fails to take into account that not everyone is "superhuman and rich," as Anne-Marie Slaughter, a Princeton professor and former senior adviser to Secretary of State Hillary Clinton, wrote in *Fortune* magazine.

Kefalas said it a little more succinctly: Sandberg lives in a fantasy world.

"We don't live in a vacuum," she said, "Maybe Sheryl does, but not the rest of us."

Moms and Dads, 1965–2011: Roles Converge, but Gaps Remain

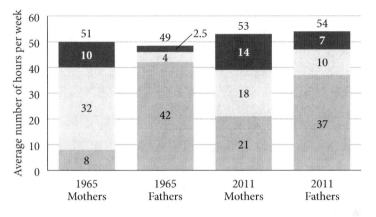

Note: Based on adults ages 18–64 with own child(ren) under age 18 living in the household. Total figures (at the top of each bar) may not add to component parts due to rounding.
Source: 1965 data from Table 5A.1-2 in Bianchi, et al. (2006).
2011 data from Pew Research analysis of the American Time Use Survey.

- Paid work
- Housework
- Child care

TAKEN FROM: Amy S. Choi, "Chart of the Day: Today's Working Moms Devote More Time to Child Care than in the '60s," *Feministing*, March 15, 2013.

She Works Hard for the Money

Put aside Sandberg's dream of more women reaching the top rungs of the corporate ladder for a moment. Statistics indicate that women still have a lot of barriers to just earning pay equal to that of their male counterparts.

Today, more than seven out of 10 mothers taking care of children are in the labor force, and nearly half of all married couples are dual breadwinners, according to Pew Research Center data from 2010.

Still, the public remains conflicted about the impact working mothers have on their young children, with only 21% of Americans saying it's a good thing.

"The cultural story of good mothering has not been reconciled yet to reflect working women," Kefalas said. "There are social rules and the standards are very demanding."

There is a structural reality that women live in, and there's a story women tell themselves about their lives—a story that is impossible to live up to, Kefalas said.

"There is no way to have it all."

Sandberg agrees. The book excerpt says women should "stop trying to have it all." It also acknowledges the "sacrifices and hardships" that are tougher today "because of the expansion of working hours."

But according to the Facebook executive, that doesn't mean working moms should give up on their careers.

"If more women lean in, we can change the power structure of our world and expand opportunities," she wrote. "Shared experience forms the basis of empathy and, in turn, can spark the institutional changes we need. More female leadership will lead to fairer treatment for all women."

Sounds easy enough, right? Not so fast, Kefalas said.

"At the end of the day, we make choices about the kind of people we want to be, and it's so much more than self-sabotaging."

> *"What makes* Lean In *valuable . . . is that it provides a series of prompts for those of us who are still figuring out what we want and what we can handle, and advice for asking for . . . it in a world that often punishes women for behaving like men."*

Leaning In Promotes Women's Solidarity

Alyssa Rosenberg

Alyssa Rosenberg is a pop culture blogger for the Washington Post *and the former features editor for the* ThinkProgress *blog. In the following viewpoint, she praises Sheryl Sandberg's book* Lean In *for providing concrete advice for young women pursuing careers. She says that Sandberg gives women useful ways to think about work-life balance and strategies for career advancement. She especially praises Sandberg's insight that women can network and promote one another's careers, since prejudices may harm women when they promote themselves.*

Alyssa Rosenberg, "Why 'Lean In' Is Worth Reading—Particularly for Young Women," *ThinkProgress*, May 22, 2013. ThinkProgress.org. © 2013 ThinkProgress. Reproduced by permission.

As you read, consider the following questions:

1. What does Rosenberg say unfairly fueled the furor over Sandberg's book?

2. What advice did Sandberg give to Priti Choksi when recruiting her to Facebook?

3. How does Sandberg suggest that women can negotiate for salaries?

When Sheryl Sandberg's *Lean In[: Women, Work, and the Will to Lead]* was released earlier this year [2013], I, to use the oft-repurposed and much-misunderstood lingo of Sandberg herself, leaned out. The book was the subject of a feminist furor, fueled by a quotation from an interview Sandberg gave for the documentary *Makers* that was unfairly truncated to suggest that she saw herself as some sort of social visionary, and the suggestion that readers form "Lean In Circles," a sort of consciousness-raising-meets-corporate-boardroom series of study groups. The fray seemed unappealing, and besides, I'd reasoned, I was doing a decent job of leaning in, even if I haven't yet complicated my work-life balance with marriage and children.

A Business Book

But last week, a good girlfriend suggested I give *Lean In* a try, and I finished it just as Anne Applebaum published a joint review of Sandberg's book and Hanna Rosin's *The End of Men* in the *New York Review of Books*, situating Sandberg's volume squarely in the tradition of business advice books. Applebaum seems disappointed, as she puts it, that "this is not a book that belongs on the shelf alongside [feminist writers] Gloria Steinem and Susan Faludi. It belongs in the business section," and maybe given some of the hype around *Lean In*, that's fair. I'm more than willing to grant that the book has many of the flaws that have been ascribed to it, including a failure to extensively discuss the role of paid help in Sandberg's work-life balance, the fact that the book is not particularly applicable to working-class women, and its cursory treatment of women in the third world. But if you are a woman preparing to begin a white-collar job, or to level up from one to the next, *Lean In* is worth reading precisely as a business book, and not because it has definitive answers for every situation, but as a useful guide for thinking through situations where there is no clear or easy answer—particularly those where women face social obstacles particular to their gender.

Applebaum's critique of *Lean In* as business advice—separate from her criticisms of Sandberg's argument that women in business leadership will create a more supportive environment for the women coming up behind them—has three central tenets. First, that Sandberg's advice appears contradictory, suggesting that women speak more at some times and less at others, or arguing for women to project confidence they don't feel in some situations, while being emotionally honest in others. Second, she argues that Sandberg doesn't provide enough specific detail about her child care arrangements for other women to model. And finally, Applebaum suggests that Sandberg hasn't given enough room to discuss factors like luck and her ability to get along with difficult men, like former Treasury secretary and longtime Sandberg mentor Larry Summers. Those last two criticisms aren't unreasonable, and it would be fascinating to read Sandberg's advice for dealing with Summers, but it's hard to see how knowing precisely how many nannies Sandberg hires would help those of us who don't have her financial resources. And I think Sandberg would have no disagreement with Applebaum's argument that:

> In practice, a successful woman—like a successful man—must learn, early on, how much emotion to show and how much to conceal, depending on the circumstances. She must learn how much to speak and how much to keep silent, for that depends on the circumstances too. Above all, she must

understand herself well enough to know which challenges are worth accepting and which—given her personal situation, her husband, her finances, her interests, her age—must be sensibly refused.

Advice for Women

What makes *Lean In* valuable, particularly for women at the earlier stages of those careers, is that it provides a series of prompts for those of us who are still figuring out what we want and what we can handle, and advice for asking for . . . it in a world that often punishes women for behaving like men. *Lean In* is significantly anecdotal, but those anecdotes serve less as hard and fast rules, and more as thought experiments. In one example, Sandberg relates the advice she gave to Priti Choksi when she was trying to recruit the younger woman to join Facebook:

> I explained that although it was counterintuitive, right before having a child can actually be a great time to take a new job. If she found her new role challenging and rewarding, she'd be more excited to return to it after giving birth. If she stayed put, she might decide that her job was not worth the sacrifice. Priti accepted our offer. By the time she started at Facebook, she was already expecting. Eight months later, she had her baby, took four months off, and came back to a job she loved. She later told me that if I had not raised the topic, she would have turned us down.

That's an idea that may have occurred to women who have already had the experience of having a child and returning to the workforce, as Sandberg did. (In what appears to be a misreading of Sandberg's definition of leaning in, Applebaum says that Sandberg leaned out for taking a real maternity leave when she had her second child, when Sandberg explains that embracing maternity leave made it easier for her to come back to the job.) But it's a way of framing that particular question that puts aside concerns about whether a woman might look less than committed for taking maternity leave early in a new job, and emphasizes what will make a woman feel energized, encouraged, and engaged instead.

Similarly, Sandberg suggests a different way to look at the cost of child care. Rather than considering nannying or preschool costs as a dilemma, something that wipes out a woman's earnings, or that's discretionary spending to allow a woman to continue doing something that she likes, Sandberg once again reframes the question, acknowledging that "child care is a huge expense, and it's frustrating to work hard just to break even. But professional women need to measure the cost of child care against their future salary rather than their current salary. . . . Wisely, . . . women have started to think of paying for child care as a way of investing in their families' future." Again, I don't blame any working woman who's already made these calculations and reached this conclusion for not finding Sandberg's advice helpful. But for young women, like the one who Sandberg describes quizzing her on work-life balance issues even though she wasn't pregnant—it turns out she didn't even have a boyfriend—these kinds of examples are a useful early intervention.

Negotiating

And beyond the question of balancing work and family, an issue that only comes into play for many women once they've already put significant work into their careers, Sandberg's case studies are useful advice for women who are already on board to lean in, but understand that they can be penalized for that desire. Sandberg's clear that she understands it's on some level unproductive to continue asking women to play by rules that reward men and punish women for the same behavior, but she suggests that it's better to give women tools that will allow them to succeed now, rather than to wait for a perfect world. . . .

Power of Women

I've had the joy of seeing women make stunning progress during my four decades of activism. Now I want to encourage women to embrace their power in this amazing moment when we can lead and live without limits. For the first time in history . . . we have the potential to do that. There are big challenges, to be sure. For example, the White House Project's benchmark study, released in December 2009, documents that women are stuck at around 18 percent of leadership positions across the ten sectors they studied. Nevertheless, the biggest question is what we will choose to do with that information.

We can start by changing the very meaning of power from an oppressive *power-over* to an expansive concept I call the *power-to.* And if we muster the courage to stand in our power and walk with intention, we can achieve our highest aspirations at work, in civic life, and in love for good—by which I mean we can transform power relationships for our own good and create good in the world for others.

But here's our predicament: Though insidious cultural barriers remain, we must face the fact that from the boardroom to the bedroom, from public office to personal relationships, no law or formal barrier is keeping us from achieving equality and justice except our own unwillingness to "just take them," as [early feminist and abolitionist] Sojourner Truth urged a century and a half ago.

Gloria Feldt,
No Excuses: Nine Ways Women Can
Change How We Think About Power.
Berkeley, CA: Seal Press, 2010.

"I have advised many women to preface negotiations by explaining that they know that women often get paid less than men so they are going to negotiate rather than accept the original offer," Sandberg advises. "By doing so, women position themselves as connected to a group and not just out for themselves; in effect, they are negotiating for all women. And as silly as it sounds, pronouns matter. Whenever possible, women should substitute 'we' for 'I.'" She also suggests that women take advantage of that expectation that they'll be concerned with others rather than with themselves. Sandberg gives this example:

> In 2004, four female executives at Merrill Lynch started having lunch together once a month. They shared their accomplishments and frustrations. They brainstormed about business. After the lunches, they would all go back to their offices and tout one another's achievements. They couldn't brag about themselves, but they could easily do it for their colleagues. Their careers flourished and each rose up the ranks to reach managing director and executive officer levels. The queen bee was banished, and the hive became stronger.

In journalism, that's the guiding principle behind sites like Lady Journos or the newly launched Journos of Color, outlets that spotlight the work of female and nonwhite writers in part so they don't have to promote themselves on their own. Sandberg may not have definitive proof that women executives make the workplace better for all women simply by their presence. But among the other advice *Lean In* gives to women, the argument it makes is that if women lean in, we don't have to do it alone, or in competition with other women as a class. Given all the expectations and double standards women face in a business environment, that's a welcome challenge to stereotype—and a suggestion that women have strength, resources, and flexibility we may not be taking advantage of.

> "What if gender difference turns out to be a phenomenon not of oppression, but rather of social well-being?"

Leaning In Ignores Women's Noncareer Goals

Christina Hoff Sommers

Christina Hoff Sommers is a resident scholar at the American Enterprise Institute; she is the author of The War Against Boys: How Misguided Feminism Is Harming Our Young Men. *In the following viewpoint, she argues that women are less career oriented than men because women are naturally more interested in home and family than in careers. She points to studies showing that industrialized countries have greater gender-role splits, suggesting that as people become wealthier and more self-actualized, women tend to move toward more traditional female roles. Sommers concludes that women may not lean in to their careers because they don't want to and prefer to pursue family-oriented goals.*

As you read, consider the following questions:

1. What are "Lean In Circles," according to Sommers?

2. What does Sommers say are the gender disparities in engineering, and what does she suggest might be the cause?

3. According to Sommers, what do poll data show about the ideal work preferences of women and men?

There is much to admire in Sheryl Sandberg's book *Lean In: Women, Work, and the Will to Lead.* It is full of funny stories about her brilliant career and helpful advice for workplace success. As former chief of staff at the U.S. Treasury Department and vice president of Google, and now COO [chief operating officer] of Facebook, the 43-year-old billionaire and mother of two has a lot of worldly wisdom to share. She is right that many women sell themselves short and pull back too early from their careers. Sandberg urges them to man up.

The Problem with 1970s Feminism

But this otherwise likeable and inspirational self-help book has a serious flaw: It is mired in 1970s-style feminism. *Nation* magazine columnist Katha Pollitt compares Sandberg to "someone who's just taken Women's Studies 101 and wants to share it with her friends." What Pollitt intends as a compliment goes to the heart of what is wrong with *Lean In.*

Sandberg envisions a time where gender roles all but disappear. "A truly equal world would be one where women ran half our countries and companies and men ran half our homes." She blames society for tricking little girls into liking princesses and little boys into preferring superheroes. "The gender stereotypes introduced in childhood are reinforced throughout our lives and become self-fulfilling prophesies."

Sandberg excels at the forward edge of economics and technology, but her sociology leans back to the Age of Aquarius. She praises to the skies Marlo Thomas's 1972 unisex album *Free to Be . . . You and Me.* She wants to bring back consciousness-raising groups, calling them "Lean in Circles."

Women are advised to meet together and carry out "Listen, ask, and share" exercises. Sandberg's "Lean In" website provides "exploration kits" for these séances. One instructs group members to go round the room and finish sentences like "What I am most looking forward to in the month ahead . . ." and "Today I am feeling . . . ." Is this how Mark Zuckerberg got to the top?

Sandberg's goal is to liberate her fellow Americans from the stereotypes of gender. But is that truly liberating? In a 2008 study in the *Journal of Personality and Social Psychology*, a group of international researchers compared data on gender and personality across 55 nations. Throughout the world, women tend to be more nurturing, risk averse and emotionally expressive, while men are usually more competitive, risk taking, and emotionally flat. But the most fascinating finding is this: Personality differences between men and women are the largest and most robust in the more prosperous, egalitarian, and educated societies. According to the authors, "Higher levels of human development—including long and healthy life, equal access to knowledge and education, and economic wealth—were the main nation-level predictors of sex difference variation across cultures." *New York Times* science columnist John Tierney summarized the study this way: "It looks as if personality differences between men and women are smaller in traditional cultures like India's or Zimbabwe's than in the Netherlands or the United States. A husband and a stay-at-home wife in a patriarchal Botswanan clan seem to be more alike than a working couple in Denmark or France."

More Actualization, More Difference

Why should that be? The authors of the study hypothesize that prosperity and equality bring greater opportunities for self-actualization. Wealth, freedom, and education empower men and women to be who they are. It is conspicuously the case that gay liberation is a feature of advanced, prosperous societies: but such societies also afford heterosexuals more opportunities to embrace their gender identities. This cross-cultural research is far from conclusive, but it is intriguing and has great explanatory power. Just think: What if gender difference turns out to be a phenomenon not of oppression, but rather of social well-being?

Consider, in this regard, the gender disparities in engineering. An article on the Wharton School website laments the paucity of women engineers and holds up China and Russia as superior examples of equity. According to the post, "In China, 40 percent of engineers are women, and in the former USSR, women accounted for 58 percent of the engineering workforce." The author blames workplace biases and stereotypes for the fact that women in the United States earn only 20 percent of the doctoral degrees in engineering. But perhaps American women earn fewer degrees in engineering because they don't have to. They have more opportunities to pursue careers that really interest them. American women may be behind men in engineering, but they now earn a majority of all PhDs and outnumber men in humanities, biology, social sciences, and health sciences. Despite 40 years of consciousness-raising and gender-neutral pronouns, most men and women still gravitate to different fields and organize their lives in different ways. Women in countries like Sweden, Norway and Iceland enjoy elaborate supportive legislation, yet their vocational preferences and family priorities are similar to those of American women.

Self-Determination

In a 2013 national poll on modern parenthood, the Pew Research Center asked mothers and fathers to identify their "ideal" working arrangement. Fifty percent of mothers said they would prefer to work part time and 11 percent said they would prefer not to work at all. Fathers answered differently:

Problems with Feminism

All indications are that the new crop of young feminist ideologues coming out of our nation's colleges are even angrier, more resentful, and more indifferent to the truth than their mentors.

The large majority of women, including the majority of college women, are distancing themselves from this anger and resentfulness. Unfortunately, they associate these attitudes with feminism, and so they conclude that they are not really feminists. According to a 1992 *Time/ CNN* poll, although 57 percent of the women responding said they believed there was a need for a strong women's movement, 63 percent said they do not consider themselves feminists. . . .

In effect, the gender feminists lack a grassroots constituency. They blame a media "backlash" for the defection of the majority of women. But what happened is clear enough: The gender feminists have stolen "feminism" from a mainstream that had never acknowledged their leadership.

Christina Hoff Sommers,
Who Stole Feminism?: How Women Have Betrayed Women.
New York: Simon & Schuster, 1995.

75 percent preferred full-time work. *And the higher the socioeconomic status of women, the more likely they were to reject full-time employment.* Among women with annual family incomes of $50,000 or higher, only 25 percent identified full-time work as their ideal. Sandberg regards such attitudes as evidence of women's fear of success, double standards, gender bias, sexual harassment, and glass ceilings. But what if they are the triumph of prosperity and opportunity?

Sandberg seems to believe that the choices of contemporary American women are not truly free. Women who opt out or "lean back" (that is, towards home) are victims of sexism and social conditioning. "True equality will be achieved only when we all fight the stereotypes that hold us back." But aren't American women as self-determining as any in the history of humanity? In place of bland assertion, Sandberg needs to explain why the life choices of educated, intelligent women in liberal, opportunity-rich societies are unfree. And she needs to explain why the choices she promotes will make women happier and more fulfilled.

An up-to-date manifesto on women and work should steer clear of encounter groups and boys-must-play-with-dolls rhetoric. It should make room for human reality: That in the pursuit of happiness, men and women often take different paths. Gender differences can sometimes be symptoms of oppression and subordination. But in a modern society, they can also be the felicitous consequences of liberated choice—of the "free to be you and me" that women have been working toward for generations.

*"Achievement at the highest level re-
quires trade-offs, whether you are male
or female."*

Leaning In Shows Success Is About Individual Choices

Christine Rosen

*Christine Rosen is a Schwartz Fellow at the New America Foun-
dation and senior editor of the* New Atlantis. *In the following
viewpoint, she praises Sheryl Sandberg's book* Lean In *for arguing that women need to be responsible for their career success.
Feminism, Rosen says, has told women that they are being
treated unfairly and that they should expect institutions to help
them self-actualize. Rosen says these ideas are unhelpful. Instead,
she praises Sandberg for insisting that women need to focus on
their careers, acknowledge their choices, and take positive steps to
attain success.*

As you read, consider the following questions:

1. Who is Abraham Maslow, and what does he say about human needs, according to Rosen?

2. What ideas about mentorship does Sandberg criticize?

Christine Rosen, "In Praise of Sheryl Sandberg," *Commentary*, May 1, 2013. © 2013 Commentary. Reproduced by permission.

3. What does Sandberg say was her single most important career decision?

In his 1943 paper, "A Theory of Human Motivation," the psychologist Abraham Maslow outlined what he called our "hierarchy of needs." Using the image of a pyramid, Maslow described its base as human beings' physiological needs (such as food and shelter), on top of which came our needs for security, for healthy social relationships, for esteem from others, and finally, at the apex, the need for self-actualization, which included such things as creativity, problem solving, and morality. The story of our lives is the story of our progression through this hierarchy, Maslow believed, and we were not all destined to reach the top. "The story of the human race is the story of men and women selling themselves short," he observed.

Work Harder

Maslow's particular brand of humanistic psychology is no longer in fashion, but it lives on in diluted form in the advice and self-help industry, whose latest purveyor is Sheryl Sandberg, chief operating officer of Facebook and author of *Lean In: Women, Work, and the Will to Lead.* Like Maslow, Sandberg is concerned with people reaching their full potential. Like him, she draws on elite examples to make her case: Maslow was partial to Albert Einstein and Gandhi, while Sandberg prefers former economic official and Harvard president Lawrence [Larry] Summers and Facebook founder Mark Zuckerberg. Unlike Maslow, Sandberg's message is targeted specifically to women.

The message is both bracing and long overdue. While she acknowledges that barriers to women's success still exist in the workplace, Sandberg focuses on something else: the fact that women aren't exhibiting as much ambition as their male counterparts. And Sandberg thinks she knows the reason why: "We hold ourselves back in ways both big and small, by lacking self-confidence, by not raising our hands, and by pulling back when we should be leaning in," she writes. "Getting rid of these internal barriers is critical to gaining power." In other words, ladies, stop curling up at the end of your workday with your Tension Tamer herbal tea and your perceived slights and your fantasies of a mentor who will sweep you off your feet and into the executive suite. Work harder. Put yourself forward. Stop using the future possibility of children as an excuse to check out of your career when it's just getting started. Self-actualization is possible, Sandberg suggests, but you have to take responsibility for pursuing it. And you can't do that with advice gleaned from *Eat, Pray, Love*; instead, think *Strive, Work, Achieve.* As a friend of mine who owns her own business said with a sigh of relief after reading the book, "Bossiness is back!"

Of course, women who don the bossy boots are guaranteed criticism for doing so, and Sandberg has been getting it from all sides. Conservatives have chastised her (correctly) for uncritically endorsing outdated feminist assumptions like the notion that an ideal world is one that achieves perfect equality between men and women in all parts of life. And culturally conservative critics have faulted her for failing to consider the needs of the children of ambitious dual-income couples and for downplaying what they believe is the unique role that mothers play in society.

On the other end of the spectrum, feminists and socially liberal critics (many of whom are themselves members of the elite) have suddenly discovered their populist pitchforks and begun waving them at Sandberg's supposed hypocrisy in offering advice to working women when she herself has so much wealth and so many resources at her disposal. And economic leftists have condemned her uncritical acceptance of the increasingly harsh demands of capitalism on its elites.

Choices and Blame

It's easy to focus on Sandberg's privileged perch and, quite frankly, to envy her ability to summon armies of nannies and housekeepers, even though she acknowledges them up front and with great appreciation. But it is harder to find fault with her assertion that all these choices have consequences, hers as much as everyone else's. She admits that because of her own ambitions and work schedule she has "missed a level of detail" about her children's lives, and she confesses that she "always wants to do more" for them. Sandberg is honest about her ambivalent feelings while also taking responsibility for the choices she has made (rather than casting about for others to alleviate the consequences of them). Her tone harks back to self-help manuals of previous eras, before everything was Oprah-fied and politicized, and authors hoped to cultivate some grit in their readers rather than leave them wallowing in victimhood. Reading her book, I felt as if the weight of a thousand scented candles and New Age bromides had suddenly been lifted. Sandberg is like the lovechild of [19th-century feminist] Susan B. Anthony and [self-help expert] Dale Carnegie with a heavy dose of 21st-century business acumen thrown in.

Her sensibility makes her something of an outlier among her peer group. Sandberg's generation was raised on the messages of second-wave feminists, many of whom made it to the top of fields that were sparsely populated with other women at the time. Their hope and expectation was that the next generation—Sandberg's—would follow eagerly along the path they forged and thus break the patriarchy's grip on power. That didn't happen, and as Sandberg recalls, she and her peers had to endure many boulevard-of-broken-dreams speeches like the one she heard from Judith Rodin, president of the Rockefeller Foundation: "My generation fought so hard to give all of you choices. We believe in choices. But choosing to leave the workforce was not the choice we thought so many of you would make." Rodin's generation of feminists very much needed a villain to help them make sense of this story: Who or what had done this terrible thing to all of these promising young women?

How unpleasant it must be, then, to hear one of those women say: Maybe *we're* the problem. For them, Sandberg is committing the cardinal sin of blaming the victim. And although she gives an obligatory nod to the arguments about flex time, maternity and paternity leave, and the like, she is more interested in exploring the consequences of women's own choices. Achievement at the highest level requires trade-offs, whether you are male or female, and Sandberg's candor in describing her own only makes the force of her argument more challenging to the feminist notion that the problem can never be attributed to us (the women), but *them* (the men, the institutions they run, the government). The black-and-white, Manichean universe of female oppression and male domination in the workplace starts to look a lot grayer after reading Sandberg's book.

Take Initiative

Even more appalling to feminist sensibilities, Sandberg suggests that women embrace some of the techniques that have proven so successful for men: Take credit for your work; sit at the table; stop apologizing for yourself and indulging your feelings of self-doubt; quit making excuses. "Taking initiative pays off," Sandberg writes. "It is hard to visualize someone as a leader if she is always waiting to be told what to do." But this supremely rational advice directly undermines a key part of the feminist message about women in leadership: the idea that it is the workplace (and men) who should conform to women's ways of doing things (which are, it is always assumed, superior to men's). Sandberg notes the contradictory messages women receive: Be aggressive, but not too aggressive; be nice, but not a doormat. But instead of blaming this situation on a patriarchal corporate conspiracy, she acknowledges the frustration of this unfair reality and then does the unthinkable: She offers advice. Yes, aggressive women are seen as unlikable even when men acting the same way are not (social science research has shown this time and time again). So use *we* instead of *I* when negotiating that raise. Be nice but also be insistent. Smile.

Is this fair in an existential sense? Of course not. But who said life is fair? How many men in the workplace feign an interest in golf or pretend to appreciate their boss's sense of humor in order to get ahead? Sandberg suggests resisting "Tiara Syndrome," a phrase coined by the founders of a women's consulting group to describe how women "expect that if they keep doing their job well someone will notice them and place a tiara on their head." Instead, she advises, take some initiative, even if the system you are working in isn't ideal.

Tiara Syndrome isn't the only myth Sandberg properly pummels. She also takes on what might be called the "Mentor Myth." As Sandberg tells it, young women in the workplace view the perfect female mentor just as little girls envision glittery rainbow-colored unicorns: powerful creatures whom they have only to discover for their lives to change forever. Sandberg recounts the many times that young women who are complete strangers have come up to her after speeches or meetings asking her to be their mentor. "The question is a total mood killer," she says. She has the wit to admit that "we've brought this on ourselves" with incessant and boosterish encouragement of the idea that young women need female role models and advisers. You can't throw a brick in the feminist community without hitting a female leadership academy (Gloria Steinem and Naomi Wolf each founded one). But Sandberg is withering in her criticism of this notion, comparing these young women's attitudes with that of Sleeping Beauty: "Now young women are told that if they can just find the right mentor, they will be pushed up the ladder and whisked away to the corner office to live happily ever after. Once again, we are teaching women to be too dependent on others."

Mentors and Mean Girls

Sandberg is not criticizing mentorship; throughout the book, she is generous and unstinting in her praise of the people whose advice and counsel helped her get ahead. What she resists is the notion, inculcated in a generation of young women raised on the drumbeat of Girl Power, that you deserve a mentor simply by showing up and having ovaries. And she notes the tendency among these young women to assume that the mentor's role is to devote herself to the care and nurturing of the mentee. After helping a bright woman rising through the ranks at Google (where Sandberg worked before moving to Facebook), she confessed to some surprise when the woman claimed never to have benefited from the guidance of a mentor. When Sandberg asked what her idea of a mentor was, the woman responded that it was someone she would talk to about her career for an hour a week. "I smiled," Sandberg writes, "thinking, *That's not a mentor—that's a therapist.*"

Many of Sandberg's mentors were men (such as [economist] Larry Summers, for whom she worked during the [Bill] Clinton administration), and this, too, rankles her critics, several of whom have implied that her sponsorship by men (and continued success in the male-dominated tech industry) casts doubt on her credentials as a card-carrying member of the sisterhood. But it is her position as an outlier in her field that makes her insights persuasive. Sandberg paints an ambiguous yet more compelling portrait of female leadership, one that resonates because she has exercised leadership herself. As for uniquely female styles of leadership, however often they reign in specific instances, history and common sense suggest they are more fiction than reality in the aggregate. (I worked for an all-female organization for many years, and I can attest, *Lord of the Flies* [a novel about children who revert to savagery on an island] had nothing on that office environment.)

Sandberg even wades into the roiling waters of women's complex feelings about other women—the "mean girl" problem, for lack of a better term. If you spend much time perusing feminist literature about women in power, you would assume that older women in the corner office are all waiting with open and nurturing arms to embrace the next bright young female thing rising through the ranks. But as Sandberg suggests, sisterhood isn't always powerful; all too often it's simply pettily vindictive. Case in point: Current Yahoo CEO [chief executive officer] Marissa Mayer, who had the audacity not only to accept that high-powered position when she was pregnant, but also to be utterly transparent about her plans for working almost immediately after the birth of her child. A nurturing world of feminist leaders should have embraced such a decision, both for its honesty and its trailblazing. Instead, Sandberg writes: "The attacks on Marissa for her maternity-leave plans came almost entirely from other women. This has certainly been my experience too."

Perhaps the best piece of advice Sandberg offers is personal, and it reads like something out of a Jane Austen novel (not the prose, of course): "I truly believe that the single most important career decision that a woman makes is whether she will have a life partner and who that partner is." This is a far cry from Gloria Steinem's tossed-off observation that "a woman without a man is like a fish without a bicycle"; indeed, Sandberg makes it clear throughout the book how crucial her husband has been to her own success and her ability to juggle an ambitious career and a family. Even when Sandberg is encouraging men to "lean in to their families" by helping more with domestic tasks, she doesn't spare women criticism. She notes how often women engage in "maternal gatekeeping" behaviors, asking husbands to take on domestic tasks but then behaving in a critical or controlling way when they perform them (in the nonacademic literature, this is known by its more familiar term, "nagging").

Choose Growth

Taken together, Sandberg's advice makes a compelling case for the argument that, contra decades of feminist propagandizing, female self-actualization is not and should not be the goal of businesses. Equal pay? Equal rights under the law? Benefits and flexibility that allow all parents to have more balanced lives? Absolutely. But a world that requires Abraham Maslow's hierarchy of needs on the corporate spreadsheet? No thanks. Sandberg's *Lean In* stands as a necessary corrective to a feminist movement that has migrated away from the pursuit of concrete political goals toward the pursuit of gauzier things like self-actualization. Women should abandon the notion that they can or should "have it all." As Sandberg correctly notes: "The greatest trap ever set for women was the coining of this phrase."

Sandberg reminds us that women can do a great deal to improve their own lives at the individual level, whether that is speaking up at a meeting or taking seriously the challenge of finding a good life partner. But she worries that "women will continue to sacrifice being liked for being successful." She insists that, to the contrary, "taking risks, choosing growth, challenging ourselves, and asking for promotions (with smiles on our faces, of course) are all important elements of managing a career." She is cruel to be kind, but in the right measure, as the 70s-era pop song goes. Fifty years after Betty Friedan told women what they suspected but couldn't articulate in *The Feminine Mystique*, Sheryl Sandberg, in her charmingly stoic way, is telling us what we know but won't admit. In this, her advice echoes that of a more traditional (and ancient) Stoic who was also a wise leader. In his *Meditations*, Marcus Aurelius advised: "Don't go on discussing what a good person should be. Just be one."

Periodical and Internet Sources Bibliography

The following articles have been selected to supplement the diverse views presented in this chapter.

Margaret Barthel	"I Wasn't a Fan of Sheryl Sandberg—Until I Couldn't Find a Job," *Atlantic*, April 8, 2014.
Lisa Bonos	"A Year After 'Lean In,' These Are Sheryl Sandberg's Truest Believers," *Washington Post*, March 7, 2014.
Meghan Casserly	"Sheryl Sandberg's 'Lean In' More Aspirational than Inspirational," *Forbes*, August 31, 2012.
Vanessa Garcia	"Why I Won't Lean In," *Huffington Post*, July 19, 2013.
Jessica Grose	"Sheryl Sandberg's 'Lean In' Circles Completely Miss the Point on Workplace Maternity," *Slate*, February 22, 2013.
Colleen Leahey	"Why the 'Lean In' Conversation Isn't Enough," *Fortune*, October 17, 2013.
Meredith Lepore	"Here's What 'Lean In' Is and Why You Should Be a Part of It," Levo League, March 10, 2013.
Kate Losse	"Feminism's Tipping Point: Who Wins from Leaning In?," *Dissent*, March 26, 2013.
Jody Greenstone Miller	"The Real Women's Issue: Time," *Wall Street Journal*, March 11, 2013.
Erin Nelson	"We Don't Need to 'Lean In,' We Need to Dismantle," *Blue Review*, April 13, 2014.
Sheryl Sandberg	"Why I Want Women to Lean In," *Time*, March 7, 2013.

CHAPTER 4

How Does Workplace Harassment Affect Working Women?

Chapter Preface

One of the most prominent discussions of workplace harassment recently has involved sexual harassment of women in the military. Military sexual harassment and rape have been characterized as an "epidemic" by numerous commenters, including Joachim Hagopian in a March 23, 2014, article at the GlobalResearch website. Hagopian says that one in three women in the military is assaulted, which is double the rate of sexual assault among the civilian population. Hagopian also says that reporting rates of sexual assault in the military are only 14 percent, and several reports highlight the fact that many officers placed in charge of programs to reduce sexual assault have themselves been accused of committing such acts. Hagopian concludes,

> This abhorrent attitude and behavior has not changed in the forty years since I was a US Army officer. I observed it alive and well at West Point as a cadet attending hops, the dances the US Military Academy sponsors for its Corps of Cadets and young co-eds in the outlying local area. I distinctly recall what cadets referred to as "pig pool contests" where a group of cadets would agree to participate in a chauvinistic and degrading competition where each cadet would attempt to locate the ugliest girl at the hop and ask her to dance. After the dance all the "good ol' boys" would gather round to vote on the ugliest girl chosen and reward the cadet who dared to dance with her $10 from each contest loser. I was appalled by this inhumane treatment and utter contempt for women, but based on observable events in the armed forces today, it appears that nothing much is changing. The culture of disrespect toward women as the prevailing attitude and exploitive, aggressive, criminal behavior against women so reprehensible then is still obviously being pathologically acted out today.

Other writers have argued, however, that the sexual assault problem in the military has been exaggerated. Rosa Brooks writing for *Foreign Policy* on July 10, 2013, says that sexual assault in the military is "a genuine and serious problem" but adds that "the frantic rhetoric may be doing more harm than good." Brooks says that rates of sexual assault in the military are actually *lower* than those in the civilian population, and she says that military personnel are more likely to report assault than are civilians. In particular, she says that rates of sexual assault in college seem to be higher than those in the military, possibly because young people (in or out of the military) are most likely to commit and experience sexual assault. Brooks concludes that "the military seems to be doing something right, since it has been able to bring sexual assault rates down below those prevalent in comparable civilian populations."

The following chapter examines other issues involving workplace harassment, including discussions of whether harassment of women is rising or falling. Additional topics focus on the sexual harassment of male employees by women, as well as the harassment experienced by women in low-wage jobs and women of color.

> *"I do not want to work anyplace where I'm humiliated, creeped out, or more focused on fending off sexual advances than I am at doing my job."*

Workplace Harassment of Women Is a Serious Problem

Jessica Wakeman

Jessica Wakeman is a staff writer at the Frisky website. In the following viewpoint, she argues that sexual harassment in the workplace should be treated seriously. She says definitions of sexual harassment are clear and straightforward. Some argue that preventing sexual harassment will result in dull workplaces, or that it victimizes men for making jokes. Wakeman says that this is false and that there is a difference between being funny and irreverent and harassing or abusing coworkers. She said the line is not difficult to see, and she concludes that tact and manners in the workplace are not a burden.

As you read, consider the following questions:

1. For what is Katie Roiphe best known, according to Wakeman?

Jessica Wakeman, "Katie Roiphe's NYT Op-Ed Dismissive That Sexual Harassment Actually Exists," The Frisky, November 14, 2011. www.thefrisky.com. © 2011 The Frisky. Reproduced by permission.

2. According to the viewpoint, how does the EEOC define sexual harassment?

3. Why does Wakeman believe that women are adept at dealing with uncomfortable and hostile situations?

As my 68-year-old, Fox News–watching, Republican-voting father tells it, once upon a time you could compliment a woman in the workplace. You were allowed to say "nice dress" or "you look nice today" and it was not a big deal. Everyone would smile pleasantly and go back to clacking on their typewriters. Then the '70s came along. Hairy-pitted fists were raised and all of a sudden you were afraid to say "nice earrings" out of fear you'd be thrown in the pokey. Or, as the tone of his voice insinuated, you'd be accused of "sexual harassment."

Misrepresenting Harassment

I wish I were exaggerating this narrative, but I am not: It's a real conversation I had with my dad last weekend when we chatted about the accusations against [2012 Republican presidential candidate] Herman Cain. I also wish that the *New York Times* op-ed written by Katie Roiphe had not misrepresented sexual harassment as boneheaded-ly as my nearly-septuagenarian father does. But, sadly, that really happened also.

Katie Roiphe is an author, NYU [New York University] professor, and critic of mainstream feminism who's most well known for her 1994 nonfiction book, *The Morning After: Fear, Sex and Feminism*. The book took aim at the idea of "date rape," mocked Take Back the Night marches and accused mainstream feminists of overemphasizing the incidences of sexual assault on campus to further their own cause. She also took issue with the way she felt mainstream feminists constantly portrayed women as victims and men as rapists, which she found to be a detrimental side effect of the women's movement in general. . . .

I say all that to explain that Katie Roiphe writing about sexual harassment in the *[New York]* *Times* likely made a lot of people suspect from the get-go. . . . But even with an open-minded reading, I found Katie Roiphe's op-ed not only problematic, but intellectually lazy—which you really shouldn't be if you're writing for the *New York* freakin' *Times* op-ed page.

Roiphe used the Herman Cain accusations as a launching point, but quickly took aim at "sexual harassment" in general, writing:

> ". . . our Puritan country loves the language of sexual harassment: it lets us be enlightened and sexually conservative, modern and judgmental, sensitive and disapproving, voyeuristic and correct all at the same time."

Not in a Grey Area

The rest of the piece is just as dismissive, complaining about how sexual harassment as a concept is far too vague and "umbrella-like" and the words women are taught to use to describe it—"uncomfortable," "inappropriate," "hostile"—are too "subjective" and "slippery." She makes it sound as if any and all sexual harassment is this fuzzy grey area that's constantly entrapping poor, victimized men. Roiphe writes:

> "Feminists and liberal pundits say, with some indignation, that they are not talking about dirty jokes or misguided compliments when they talk about sexual harassment, but, in fact, they are: sexual harassment, as they've defined it, encompasses a wide and colorful spectrum of behaviors."

Yet despite alluding to a "spectrum of behaviors," she purposefully doesn't get more specific. Throughout the entire piece, she never actually says what sexual harassment is or isn't, she only complains that *other* people—she specifically quotes the American Association of University Women, unspecific sexual harassment "workshops," and Princeton's guidelines from "the '90s"—have made it too vague and complains about its vagueness. That's an entirely self-serving argument for her dismissiveness because there are, in fact, *really specific definitions* for what sexual harassment is and is not.

Definitions

As defined by the Equal Employment Opportunity Commission [EEOC], sexual harassment includes "unwanted sexual advances, requests for sexual favors, and other verbal or physical harassment of a sexual nature." It does not include "simple teasing, offhand comments, or isolated incidents." Rather, it is defined as behavior that is "so frequent or severe that it creates a hostile work environment or when it results in an adverse employment decision." You can read much more specifically about policy on sexual harassment on the EEOC web site.

It's pretty clear from that definition what sexual harassment is and what it isn't. Is that definition not specific enough for Roiphe? Does she disagree with it? Or does she just think it's not being applied as the standard definition for sexual harassment and that a more "vague" definition has taken precedent? It's unclear because Roiphe never addresses that such a specific definition does indeed *exist*.

Perhaps that's because doing so wouldn't serve Katie Roiphe's argument—that workplaces should not be "drab, cautious, civilized, quiet and comfortable." Instead, they should be "colorful," filled with "irreverence, wildness, incorrectness, ease"—and I would imagine, although she does not explicitly say it, flirtation. Here is where Katie Roiphe could benefit from her own tactic of seeing shades of grey instead of black and white. *No one* is suggesting that workplaces become staid, colorless environments filled with shivering automatons, fearful to speak up, let alone crack a joke. If a person's need to exert their power over others in the workplaces makes him feel

Herman Cain

On October 31, [2011,] *Politico* reported that two women had accused [Republican presidential candidate] Herman Cain of sexual harassment and received financial settlements from the National Restaurant Association during his tenure as president from 1996 to 1999. On November 3, a third woman came forward to accuse Cain of sexual harassment. On November 7, another woman, Sharon Bialek, accused Cain of actual sexual assault. Amid these allegations, news coverage of Cain spiked dramatically. At its peak, almost 75% of all mentions of the Republican candidates were mentions of Cain.

These allegations brought further scrutiny of Cain's behavior and the vague and evasive answers he and his spokespersons gave to questions about the allegations. News coverage of Cain became much more negative and his poll numbers continued to drop. In the week after Bialek came forward, Cain's poll numbers averaged 19%. By the end of November, the "decline" phase was well under way. His share of news coverage had plummeted and his poll numbers had slipped further to about 15%. Cain was then hit with a fourth allegation, this one from a woman named Ginger White who claimed that she and Cain had carried on a thirteen-year affair that had ended only just before he began his presidential campaign. His news coverage spiked again, and his poll numbers fell even further. He was back to single digits in the two national polls right before he suspended his campaign on December 3.

John Sides and Lynn Vavreck,
The Gamble: Choice and Chance in the
2012 Presidential Election. *Princeton, NJ:*
Princeton University Press, 2013.

so strictly corseted by sexual harassment regulations that he "becomes a dull boy," so to speak, it sounds like he should be in therapy, not status meetings.

Likewise, *no one* is trying to legislate anyone else's sense of humor: It's possible for workplaces to still be "irreverent" and filled with "ease" without saying it is permissible to send around an email ranking the hotness of all the women in the office on a scale of 1 to 10. That kind of "humor," if you could call it that, is for after hours and if that's a problem for you then you need to deal with it. (As blogger Amanda Marcotte put it on the blog *Pandagon*, "Oh my god, the feelings of old men, no matter how rude or bigoted, must be protected at all costs.")

Rather than acknowledging that not sexually harassing people is fundamentally about affirming the dignity of other human beings and having good manners (good manners! remember that idea?), Katie Roiphe tries to make it fit into her victimization narrative. When she writes, "the majority of women in the workplace are not tender creatures and are largely adept at dealing with all varieties of uncomfortable or hostile situations," she is completely ignoring the fact that women are adept at dealing with uncomfortable and hostile situations *because we have legal protection* against them and most of us have been raised in *a society that taught us to speak up* for ourselves when we are harassed. And besides being glib, her comment, "Show me a smart, competent young professional woman who is utterly derailed by a verbal unwanted sexual advance or an inappropriate comment about her appearance, and I will show you a rare spotted owl," makes it sound as if, say, a female intern is "derailed" by the office creep repeatedly keeping her late after work, telling her she's got a great body, and propositioning her to get a drink, why, she's just too feminine and weak to handle it! Who's insulting to women now, Katie Roiphe?

Tact and Manners

The phrase that kept tossing in my head as I read—and re-read—the op-ed this weekend was, *Lady, you do not speak for me.* I, for one, am *not* too weak or feminine to handle sexual harassment. I have stood up for myself at least twice when sexually harassed at various jobs in the past. I also have a dirty mouth and a lewd sense of humor. But I also know when and with whom it's appropriate to make a joke about vaginas and when it's not.

That's called *having tact.* I do not want to work anyplace where I'm humiliated, creeped out, or more focused on fending off sexual advances than I am at doing my job.

Most women, I think, feel the same way I do. We want to be treated with dignity. We want to treat others with dignity. And we want to be left alone so we could just do our jobs. It's *not* that complicated.

> "Although the number of sexual harass-
> ment charges has gone down and Wall
> Street has grown more accommodating
> of women over time, . . . a locker-room
> mentality may still pervade."

The Truth About Sexual Harassment and Retaliation

Julie Steinberg

Julie Steinberg is a banking reporter at the Wall Street Journal.
*In the following viewpoint, she reports that sexual harassment
lawsuits have fallen in Wall Street firms, indicating that companies may be taking harassment more seriously. However, it may
also be a sign that people are less willing to file claims, perhaps
because of the poor economy and worries about losing their jobs.
Steinberg notes that claims that employers are retaliating against
those who file discrimination complaints have risen, suggesting
that problems remain.*

As you read, consider the following questions:

1. According to Steinberg, what firms have instituted tough
   antiharassment policies?

2. What does Steinberg say that women who make sexual harassment complaints risk?

3. When does Steinberg say that interest in sexual harassment issues peaked?

The workplace seems to be getting safer for women when it comes to sexual harassment.

Sexual harassment charges across 20 different industries decreased to 11,717 in 2010 from 15,475 in 2001, according to data provided by the Equal Employment Opportunity Commission (EEOC), the U.S. body that oversees discrimination laws. While the decline in sexual harassment charges could point to tougher policies in the workplace that obviate the need for federal involvement, experts say that the situation may be more complicated. Women could just be more reluctant to come forward for fear of retaliation from their employers.

Pockets of Progress

The finance, insurance and real estate industries in particular saw a significant decrease in sexual harassment charges during the last decade: 266 were filed in 2010, down from 641 in 2001. Charges filed in engineering, which includes civil engineering construction, engineering services and research and development in the physical and life sciences, decreased to 48 in 2010 from 55 in 2001.

Elizabeth Grossman, a regional attorney at the New York district office of the EEOC, said many Wall Street firms are now conducting thorough investigations into internal claims within their HR departments.

Over the past decade, Grossman said, many firms have implemented tough sexual harassment policies: Morgan Stanley, Bank of America and Goldman Sachs, for example, all claim zero tolerance for sexual harassment. All three companies said they've had policies in place "for many years"—none would specify how many—designed to address sexual harassment and discrimination claims.

While it's not required for employees to file a complaint with their company before reaching out to the EEOC, the agency recommends that they do so.

"[The decline in charges] may be due to the fact that a company has a strong HR department, everything gets corrected as soon as it's reported, and there's no reason to file an EEOC charge," Grossman said.

"Over the years, we have continued to refine and enhance our compliance programs—including providing multiple avenues for employees to report concerns or complaints—and are committed to maintaining a workplace where people of diverse backgrounds can flourish," a spokesperson for CB Richard Ellis, a real estate services company, said. "Because of this effort, we are seeing fewer filed cases as employees raise potential issues earlier through internal channels."

Wake-Up Call

The finance industry has also witnessed some high-profile harassment suits over the past decade, such as those filed against Morgan Stanley in 2007 and CB Richard Ellis in 2002.

"When that happens, that's often a wake-up call within the whole industry to get their act together," said Peggy Stockdale, a professor of applied psychology at Southern Illinois University Carbondale and an editor of *Sex Discrimination in the Workplace: Multidisciplinary Perspectives*. "More policies are put into place and there's more leadership training, which could help bring the numbers down."

Amy Siskind, a former department head of distressed debt trading at Morgan Stanley, believes that the issue of sexual harassment has been inaccurately portrayed as an industry problem. The real culprits are individual managers, not the firms themselves, she said.

"The industry itself is not flawed," said Siskind, who co-founded the New Agenda, an organization dedicated to advancing women into leadership roles. "It really comes down to who the managers are in a particular division. Some are gender-blind and some are gender-biased."

The Bad News

Although the number of sexual harassment charges has gone down and Wall Street has grown more accommodating of women over time, (see William D. Cohan's account of gender issues at Lazard in *The Last Tycoons: The Secret History of Lazard Frères & Co.*) a locker-room mentality may still pervade.

One analyst at a bulge-bracket bank who did not want to be named said senior executives from private equity firms with which she dealt would consistently stare at her chest or call her "sweetheart." In one off-putting moment, a vice president from her bank hovered over her and told her she smelled "so good," to which she replied: "Thanks, you should get this shampoo for your wife."

In traditionally male-dominated workplaces, "you often still see the remnants of the former culture," said Grossman.

The low harassment numbers could be a reflection of women's desire to stay quiet. Reporting allegations of sexual harassment entails a career risk many women may not want to take, according to employment lawyers, particularly in an economy that's still unstable and seeing layoffs. The EEOC numbers may not accurately reflect actual incidences.

"These are certainly not the numbers of people being harassed," Stockdale said. "These are people who have gone all the way to file a complaint with the EEOC. It's the tip of the iceberg."

Women who file a complaint take on the risk of losing their job, receiving a demotion, being passed over for plum assignments, and other such retaliation from their employers.

"Women are terrified to come forward because they feel vulnerable with regard to their job security," said Allegra Fishel, an attorney at Outten & Golden, a New York–based employment law firm. "When a woman comes forward and complains about sexual harassment, she loses traction in the short run, for sure, and maybe in the long run for their career success."

Retaliation Claims Rise

Employees can file a retaliation claim with the EEOC and ultimately a lawsuit against the company if they believe they are the target of retaliation by the company for having filed a discrimination complaint.

In 2010, for the first time in the EEOC's history, retaliation was the most frequently filed charge (36,258 claims). Retaliation rates in engineering rose to 195 charges filed in 2010 from 107 filed in 2001. Similarly, the number of charges in marketing, which includes marketing research, public polling and telemarketing, increased from 5 in 2001 to 55 in 2010. Finance, on the other hand, has been on a downward slope to 1,266 retaliation charges filed in 2010 from 1,662 charges filed in 2001.

An increase in retaliation claims could be tied to a Supreme Court case from 2006. In *Burlington Northern v. White*, the Supreme Court expanded the scope of what constituted a retaliation claim, concluding that "the employer's actions must be harmful to the point that they could well dissuade a reasonable worker from making or supporting a charge of discrimination."

"The Supreme Court ruling has made employees more confident about filing a charge," said Adam Klein, a partner at Outten & Golden and the co-lead plaintiffs' counsel in the gender discrimination lawsuit against Goldman Sachs. "In a bad market, employers are less willing to tolerate [discrimination] complaints, leading to more retaliatory actions, and employees are fighting back."

Cycles of Concern

Even for those who are pleased that companies have made strides on this issue over the past decade, they're not ready to relax just yet.

Public interest in sexual harassment issues tends to go in waves, peaking when cases like Anita Hill's make the front page and then receding shortly after, only to rise again when a new lawsuit comes along. (Hill was an attorney-advisor who in 1991 claimed Supreme Court Justice Clarence Thomas had made unwelcome sexual statements to her.)

"People have cycles of concern," Stockdale of Southern Illinois University Carbondale said, referring to the above phenomenon. "A downward trend does not mean that sexual harassment will go down to zero. I would hope that training and attention and good leadership practices do have a benefit, but they have to be maintained. It can't be a one-shot-in-the-arm type of approach."

"*Since sexual harassment is about power, not sex, it's not surprising that low-wage women in lousy jobs get a lot of it.*"

Sexual Harassment Remains Endemic in Low-Wage Jobs

Jane Slaughter

Jane Slaughter is a journalist who writes on labor affairs for the Labor Notes website and for magazines such as In These Times. *In the following viewpoint, she reports that sexual harassment in low-wage jobs is high. The restaurant industry has particularly high rates of sexual harassment, and women farmworkers also face serious harassment. She says that women who report harassment may be fired or face other retaliation from their employers. Nonetheless, she contends that some progress has been made and that there have been some gains in protections for female farmworkers.*

As you read, consider the following questions:

1. According to Slaughter, what well-known restaurant chains faced charges of sexual harassment?

2. According to Slaughter, under what circumstances can female farmworkers be especially vulnerable to sexual harassment?

3. What protections for workers were established by the Fair Food Code of Conduct, according to Slaughter?

Since sexual harassment is about power, not sex, it's not surprising that low-wage women in lousy jobs get a lot of it. The Equal Employment Opportunity Commission says the restaurant industry is the largest source of sexual harassment claims. And the Coalition of Immokalee Workers (CIW) [a worker-based human rights organization] finds harassment of women farmworkers to be pervasive.

Accepted

In a national survey of 4,300 restaurant workers by the . . . Restaurant Opportunities Centers United [ROC], more than one in 10 workers reported that they or a coworker had experienced sexual harassment. ROC says even this creepy figure is likely an undercount.

Focus groups and interviews ROC conducted nationwide found sexual harassment an "accepted . . . part of the culture." One worker said, "It's inevitable. If it's not verbal assault, someone wants to rub up against you."

ROC reviewed four years of EEOC sexual harassment settlements and verdicts in the restaurant industry and found that cases were filed primarily against well-known chains, including McDonald's (the worst with 16 percent of the cases), KFC, Sonic, IHOP, Applebee's, Cracker Barrel, Ruby Tuesday, and Denny's.

Most often, workers were abused and harassed daily and faced some form of retaliation for complaining.

Direct Intimidation

One farmworker described the norm in the fields similarly to that in restaurants: "You allow it or they fire you." A 2010

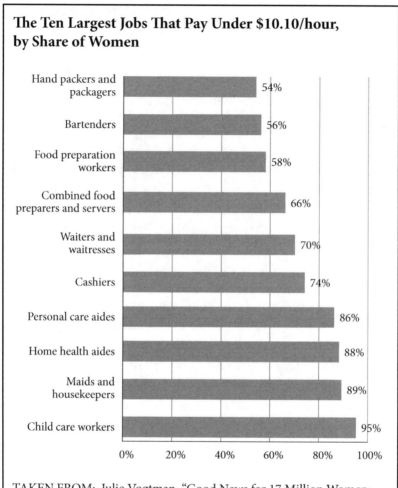

The Ten Largest Jobs That Pay Under $10.10/hour, by Share of Women

Job	Percentage
Hand packers and packagers	54%
Bartenders	56%
Food preparation workers	58%
Combined food preparers and servers	66%
Waiters and waitresses	70%
Cashiers	74%
Personal care aides	86%
Home health aides	88%
Maids and housekeepers	89%
Child care workers	95%

TAKEN FROM: Julie Vogtman, "Good News for 17 Million Women: Fair Minimum Wage Act to Be Introduced Today," National Women's Law Center, March 5, 2013.

study of farmworker women found 80 percent had experienced sexual harassment at work.

Farmworker women can be especially vulnerable when they are employed and paid by individual crew leaders, who thus have tight control over their livelihoods.

One was fired along with her husband and son, and lost their company housing, after she complained to the company's human resources office of a crew leader's uninvited visits to her trailer after her husband had left for work. The crew leader was responsible for, and often withheld, her pay.

The Fair Food Code of Conduct [that] CIW negotiated with Florida tomato growers and fast-food chains enables CIW to set up worker-to-worker trainings that address sexual harassment on company time. A "Know Your Rights" booklet and video include a sexual harassment scenario scripted and acted by CIW members.

The code has enforcement provisions, too. Sexual harassment that involves physical contact will cause curtailment of tomato purchases from participating growers for at least three months, unless the harasser is fired and other corrective action is taken.

In a report on its Fair Food Program for 2011–13, CIW reports two cases of growers who responded . . . by firing abusive crew leaders and conducting trainings.

| "Racialized sexual harassment is the way women of color are uniquely harassed in ways that combine race and gender."

Black Women Are Especially Vulnerable to Workplace Harassment

Kunbi Tinuoye

Kunbi Tinuoye is a news correspondent for MSNBC and a contributor to the Grio website. In the following viewpoint, she says that sexual harassment remains a serious problem for women in the workplace. She argues that harassment can be especially targeted at black women because racial stereotypes portray them as sexualized and inferior. Black women may also be unwilling to report harassment because of their precarious position in the job market and because of distrust of law enforcement, Tinuoye says.

As you read, consider the following questions:

1. According to the viewpoint, who is Kelley Hardwick, and what does she claim in her lawsuit?

2. According to Deborrah Cooper, why are black women singled out for sexual harassment?

Kunbi Tinuoye, "Is Sexual Harassment Different from the Perspective of Black Women?," The Grio, June 22, 2012. TheGrio.com. © 2012 The Grio. Reproduced by permission.

3. What instances of harassment does Carolyn M. West say that she faced?

Sexual harassment has been back in the news with reports of a lawsuit against . . . women's basketball coach Geno Auriemma.

Harassment Is Still Pervasive

Kelley Hardwick, an African American NBA [National Basketball Association] security official, claims Auriemma had her removed from an assignment to the 2012 London [Olympic] Games in retaliation, after she spurned his advances. In addition, she alleges she was paid less than her male counterparts and was "slammed hard" against the league's "glass ceiling."

In response, Auriemma called the claims "beyond false" and said he would defend himself "to the fullest." The employment discrimination lawsuit, filed June 11 in state supreme court in Manhattan, names Auriemma, the NBA and USA Basketball as defendants.

Whatever the outcome of this case, it is a stark reminder that sexual misconduct in the workplace is still alive and kicking, even at the highest levels.

In fact, according to the National Council for Research on Women, at least half of all women will experience sexual harassment at some point in their lives.

"Sexual harassment is still pervasive, frequent and harmful," high-profile Los Angeles attorney Gloria Allred told the Grio.

However, according to clinical psychologist Nicole T. Buchanan of Michigan State University, experts who investigate harassment have been disturbingly silent about issues facing women of color.

For African American women, sexual harassment is rarely, if ever, about sex or sexism alone; it is also about race, says

Buchanan. "Racialized sexual harassment is the way women of color are uniquely harassed in ways that combine race and gender."

Advice columnist Deborrah Cooper, who says she herself has experienced sexual harassment in corporate America, agrees that gender and ethnicity play a role in how different women are treated, or mistreated, in the workplace. "White employees tend to feel superior," coworkers are "less respectful towards black women," and there is the perception that "sistas are of less value," says Cooper.

Sexism and Racism

For Buchanan, sexual harassment is inextricably intertwined with racist attitudes. "Sometimes drawing on stereotypes of black women, for example, the assumption that African American women are hypersexual," says Buchanan.

Buchanan states that black women are more vulnerable in the workplace, not only because of cultural norms, but [also because of] economic inequality and organizational power. "Women of color tend to have less power and people with less power tend to be harassed or victimized."

"Perpetrators target people who are vulnerable, less credible or less likely to resist what's happening," says University of Washington psychology professor Dr. Carolyn M. West. "Sexual harassment isn't just about sex," says Buchanan. "It is about power, control and dominance. It's a way to put people in their place."

Black women, for instance, may remain silent when work colleagues cross the line because of their more precarious position in the job market, which may make them feel they have too much to lose by speaking out.

The race of the perpetrator is an underlying factor, says Dr. West. She says black women have a history of victimization from slavery to their role as domestic servants and even as professionals in corporate America. However, if the harasser is a black man, an African American woman may stay silent to protect him.

Cooper says African American women may also be less likely to report harassment because of a cultural resistance to law enforcement. "They don't want outsiders getting into their business."

Dr. West admits she was a victim of sexual harassment as a graduate student at the University of Missouri–St. Louis in the late 1980s. After enduring three years of systematic harassment at the hands of her supervisor, West finally found the courage to go public and take legal action.

She says she waited so long before coming forward because she was afraid her supervisor and his powerful colleagues "would end [my] career before it began by forcing [me] out of my doctoral program." West adds, "I felt haunted by the oversexed, promiscuous black Jezebel image that is common in American culture."

In addition, "I knew I wasn't his only victim. Still, I feared that my complaints wouldn't be viewed as credible," says West, who is also author of the award-winning book *Violence in the Lives of Black Women: Battered, Black and Blue.*

"Fear is a weapon that keeps most women from standing up for their rights," says Allred. They are fearful of losing their job, worried about retaliation from employers, the emotional cost and financial implications of legal fees, says Allred.

VIEWPOINT 5

| "There's a 'persistent misconception' that sexual harassment involves only male-on-female conduct."

Young Men Increasingly Complain of Workplace Violations

Laura Gunderson

Laura Gunderson is an investigative reporter for the Oregonian. *In the following viewpoint, she reports that the number of sexual harassment complaints by men has risen. She says sexual harassment can be especially difficult for young men, who may not realize that harassment of men, as well as of women, is illegal. She explains that young men may also feel that they should enjoy advances or should be able to handle such situations on their own, even though their harasser may be able to control their work schedules and pay rates.*

As you read, consider the following questions:

1. According to Gunderson, what percentage of sexual harassment complaints were filed by men in 2000 as compared to that in 2011?

2. How much in damages did Carmike Cinemas pay and to whom, according to Gunderson?

3. What sort of thinking does Erick Mertz say becomes a barrier for men who are harassed?

The first few times Tyler Kimball's male boss massaged his shoulders, touched his knee or bumped his arm, the teen shrugged it off.

As a teenager who had recently come out as homosexual, Kimball recalls thinking his boss was a "straight married man with no interest in a young boy."

Kimball, now in his mid-20s and living in Portland, still recoils as he tells the story of the day his boss walked by his chair, reached his hand up Kimball's shorts and grabbed his genitals.

"It all happened so fast," Kimball said, "I was paralyzed with shock."

Although the federal Equal Employment Opportunity Commission [EEOC] doesn't require birth dates on sexual harassment complaint forms, the agency does track gender. Most sexual harassment complaints are filed by women, yet a steadily growing number nationwide are reported by male workers.

In 2000, the EEOC and other state or municipal agencies enforcing labor laws received 15,836 sexual harassment complaints, 13.6 percent of which were filed by men. In 2011, the most recent year available, complaints dropped to 11,364, yet the percentage filed by men grew to 16.3 percent.

Some of those cases led to major EEOC lawsuits:

• Carmike Cinemas, a North Carolina–based chain that operates 251 theaters in 37 states, agreed in 2005 to pay $765,000 to 14 teenage males who reported that their supervisor made sexual advances and comments toward them. Carmike Cinemas did not admit to any wrong-doing.

- Pand Enterprises, a McDonald's franchisee that operates restaurants in New Mexico, agreed in 2006 to pay a group of teenage boys, some as young as 15, who reported their male boss groped them and made sexually offensive comments. Pand Enterprises did not admit to any wrongdoing.

- Hotel giant WorldMark by Wyndham agreed in 2008 to pay at least $370,000 to four male employees, ranging from 17 to 25 years old, who had reported their 40-year-old male boss sexually harassed them at the Birch Bay resort in Blaine, Wash. Wyndham did not admit to any wrongdoing.

The Oregon Bureau of Labor and Industries doesn't track the gender of employees who file sexual harassment complaints, but a scan of its records showed that between 30 and 40 men have filed reports each year since 2008. The high was in 2011, when about 50 men filed sexual harassment complaints—about 25 percent of the total complaints.

William R. Tamayo, an EEOC regional attorney based in San Francisco who worked on the Birch Bay resort case, said there's a "persistent misconception" that sexual harassment involves only male-on-female conduct.

"These young people need to know their labor rights," he said. "If they want to drive, we make sure they learn the safety rules. If they work, they should know the safety rules there. It needs to be a part of the civic culture."

Indeed, in an online survey about sexual harassment of young employees, readers reported to the *Oregonian* that they weren't sure the behavior was illegal and, if so, where to get help.

Sexual Harassment Complaints Filed by Men

The Equal Employment Opportunity Commission tallies the number of complaints filed by men to the federal agency and to state departments nationwide that enforce labor laws.

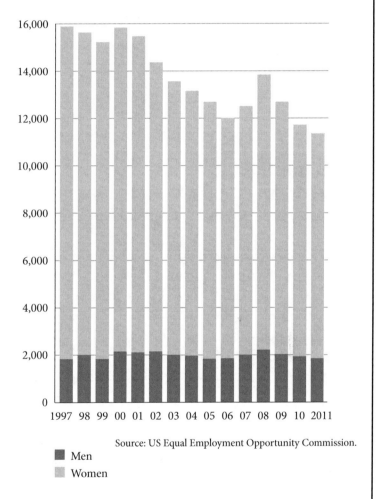

Source: US Equal Employment Opportunity Commission.

■ Men
▨ Women

TAKEN FROM: Laura Gunderson, "Young Men Increasingly Complain of Workplace Violations: Teen Sexual Harassment," OregonLive.com, April 3, 2014.

Kimball first shared his story as part of the *Oregonian*'s online survey. Of the 20 readers who filled out the survey, five were men. Some said they were confused by the behavior of their bosses and coworkers and questioned how they were supposed to react, both as an employee but also as young men in the midst of developing their sexual identity and boundaries.

They all said they shared their stories in the hope of starting conversations about the issue and letting others know they're not alone.

One man, now 30, recalled his experience at his first job at a Portland entertainment venue. The man asked to remain anonymous fearing his experience could hurt his current employment.

He was working with a woman who was a few years older and who, he said, harassed a number of his young male coworkers.

"One evening we were putting equipment away and she backed me into a corner, grabbed my package and attempted to force a kiss," he said. "I turned away from her and she realized at that point I had no interest."

He remembers feeling caught off guard. Societal pressures on teenage boys, he said, seem to suggest they should respond willingly regardless of actual interest to demonstrate sexual prowess.

Instead, he said, he felt "creeped out."

He didn't report the woman's behavior, he said, which he ignored over the next three weeks until it stopped.

As with young women, teen and 20-something men tend to work in industries that attract others their age, including entertainment venues, fast-food chains and retail stores. That can lead to a higher number of incidents of sexual harassment of young people in those particular fields.

Erick Mertz began his first job as a teenager in one of those industries. He learned how to read a schedule. How to ask for a day off. How to talk to customers. He also learned to dread the nights he'd end up working with an older female manager who he said began sexually harassing him.

He didn't complain, feeling he should be grateful for the hours and experience. In his second job many years later, he again experienced what he considered sexual harassment from another female boss.

Instead of being judged on his work, he said, the hours he'd receive—and in turn, the size of his paycheck—depended on how he reacted to her behavior. At first some of his friends joked, "Why not?" "She's not unattractive."

But then, he said, they saw how the situation was taking its toll.

He said he began to understand the stress, both mental and physical, that sexual harassment could have on a woman who must support a family or pay a mortgage. He also clearly saw how gender issues tangled up his thinking on what to do.

He didn't file a complaint, but became very cautious in his next job.

"For men, the question is when do you call it harassment?" he said. "That whole 'You're not man enough to handle it yourself' thing becomes a barrier. A few times I felt that I should have been 'man enough' to throw down the gauntlet and say 'No,' but I was not in the power position.

"Sometimes 'Man enough' doesn't come into play."

Periodical and Internet Sources Bibliography

The following articles have been selected to supplement the diverse views presented in this chapter.

Donna Ballman	"Top 10 Things You Need to Know If You're Sexually Harassed at Work," AOL Jobs, June 16, 2011.
Laura Bates	"Sexual Harassment in the Workplace Is Endemic," *Guardian*, October 23, 2013.
Jillian Berman and Emily Swanson	"Workplace Sexual Harassment Poll Finds Large Share of Workers Suffer, Don't Report," *Huffington Post*, August 27, 2013.
Katrina Bishop	"Harassment at Work: 52% of Women Report Bullying," CNBC, April 2, 2014.
Bryce Covert	"One in Five Women Have Been Sexually Harassed by a Boss," *ThinkProgress*, August 29, 2013.
Gary Langer	"One in Four U.S. Women Reports Workplace Harassment," ABC News, November 16, 2011.
Roberta Matuson	"Let's Talk About Sexual Harassment in the Workplace," *Forbes*, August 22, 2013.
Anu Passary	"2 in 3 Female Scientists Face Sexual Harassment at Workplace," *Tech Times*, July 20, 2014.
Kathleen Raven	"How Sexual Harassment Changed the Way I Work," *Nature*, December 5, 2013.
Erin Gloria Ryan	"Women Post Awful Tales of Workplace Harassment on Secret Sharing Site," *Jezebel*, July 8, 2014.
Greg Stohr	"Supreme Court Limits Workplace Harassment, Retaliation Claims," *Insurance Journal*, June 25, 2013.

For Further Discussion

Chapter 1

1. Bryce Covert claims that women are paid less than men for performing the same work. What evidence does the author cite to support her argument? What suggestions does Covert offer to end discrimination in the workplace? Do you think implementation of these suggestions would be successful? Explain your reasoning.

2. Hope Yen references a Pew Research Center report on working women. What are the findings of the report? In your opinion, what is the significance of the findings? Explain, citing text from the viewpoint to support your answer.

3. Caryl Rivers and Rosalind C. Barnett argue that attractive women experience discrimination at work. After reading the viewpoint, do you think it is fair for a woman to be fired because of her physical appearance? Explain your reasoning.

Chapter 2

1. The viewpoints in this chapter discuss working mothers. Based on the viewpoints, do you believe motherhood affects working women in a positive, negative, or neutral way? Present examples from the viewpoints to support your answer.

2. Lisa Belkin argues that studies comparing working mothers' happiness to stay-at-home mothers' happiness fail to serve their purpose. What are the author's main reasons for making this claim? Do you agree or disagree with Belkin, and why?

3. Marques Lang argues that society as a whole "must begin to realize that the gender income gap is not just a woman

or mother problem, but it is a family and cultural issue that affects everyone." What does he mean by this? Do you agree or disagree with Lang's statement? Explain your reasoning.

Chapter 3

1. The viewpoints in this chapter address the lean-in movement. After reading the viewpoints, do you think leaning in benefits working women? Cite examples from the viewpoints in the chapter to defend your answer.

2. Sheryl Sandberg explains to Cindi Leive how women can be successful in their careers. Do you think the advice Sandberg offers to women is beneficial? Can you think of any ways that Sandberg's advice to women to lean in can be harmful? Cite examples from the viewpoints in the chapter to support your answer.

3. Christine Rosen praises Sheryl Sandberg's book *Lean In*, while Christina Hoff Sommers believes that Sandberg's movement disregards most women's noncareer goals. With which author do you agree, and why?

Chapter 4

1. In her viewpoint, Jessica Wakeman cites a *New York Times* op-ed that states "the majority of women in the workplace are not tender creatures and are largely adept at dealing with all varieties of uncomfortable or hostile situations." How does Wakeman refute this claim? With which do you tend to agree—the op-ed author or Wakeman? Explain your reasoning.

2. According to Julie Steinberg, sexual harassment charges in the workplace have decreased, but the problem still remains. Why does the author believe this view to be true? Do you agree or disagree with Steinberg's view, and why?

3. Laura Gunderson claims that the number of young men experiencing sexual harassment in the workplace has in-

creased. Based on Gunderson's argument, why do you think this is a growing problem in America? Do you think men experience sexual harassment at work at the same level of frequency as women do? Explain your reasoning.

Organizations to Contact

The editors have compiled the following list of organizations concerned with the issues debated in this book. The descriptions are derived from materials provided by the organizations. All have publications or information available for interested readers. The list was compiled on the date of publication of the present volume; the information provided here may change. Be aware that many organizations take several weeks or longer to respond to inquiries, so allow as much time as possible.

9to5
207 E. Buffalo Street, Suite 211, Milwaukee, WI   53202
(414) 274-0925 • fax: (414) 272-2870
e-mail: 9to5@9to5.org
website: www.9to5.org

Founded in 1973, 9to5 is one of the largest national membership organizations of working women in the United States. It is dedicated to putting working women's issues on the public agenda and to strengthening women's ability to work for economic justice. In addition to its quarterly *Newsline* newsletter, 9to5 also publishes reports about working women, including the "2012 Annual Report—40 Years of Winning Justice for Working Women." Its website features the 9to5 Action Center, which provides up-to-date information on legislation and campaigns that impact working women and their families.

American Business Women's Association (ABWA)
9820 Metcalf Avenue, Suite 110, Overland Park, KS   66212
(800) 228-0007 • fax: (913) 660-0101
e-mail: webmail@abwa.org
website: www.abwa.org

The American Business Women's Association (ABWA) is a national organization established for working women and women business owners. Established in 1949, ABWA brings together businesswomen of diverse occupations and provides opportunities for them and others to grow personally and professionally through leadership, education, networking support, and national recognition. The organization publishes the magazine *Women in Business*, which features articles such as "Finding Success in Small Businesses."

Business and Professional Women's Foundation (BPW Foundation)

1718 M Street NW, #148, Washington, DC   20036
(202) 293-1100
e-mail: foundation@bpwfoundation.org
website: bpwfoundation.org

The Business and Professional Women's Foundation (BPW Foundation) was the first foundation dedicated to conducting research and providing information solely about working women. It is a multigenerational, nonpartisan membership organization that supports workforce development programs and workplace policies that recognize the diverse needs of working women. The organization communicates its research and objectives through issue briefs and reports, such as "Ready to Grow: A Snapshot of Women Small Business Owners."

Catalyst

120 Wall Street, 15th Floor, New York, NY   10005
(212) 514-7600 • fax: (212) 514-8470
e-mail: info@catalyst.org
website: www.catalyst.org

Catalyst is a nonprofit organization that works to expand opportunities for women in business. Formed in 1962, Catalyst conducts research on all aspects of women's career advancement and provides strategic and web-based consulting services worldwide. The organization publishes many studies and reports that are available on its website, including "Sex Discrimination and Sexual Harassment" and "Feeling Different: Being the 'Other' in US Workplaces."

The Christian Working Woman (TCWW)
PO Box 1210, Wheaton, IL   60187-1116
(630) 462-0552 • fax: (630) 462-1613
e-mail: tcww@christianworkingwoman.org
website: christianworkingwoman.org

The Christian Working Woman (TCWW) is a nonprofit organization that seeks to help working women practice the teachings of Christ in the workplace. TCWW began in 1984 at the Moody Church in Chicago, Illinois, as an outgrowth of a ministry for workplace women. The organization produces two radio programs that are heard on more than five hundred stations across the United States, provides books and materials, organizes retreats and conferences, and distributes an inspiring e-mail message daily. Its website offers many resources, including podcasts, testimonies, and transcripts of its radio broadcasts.

Coalition of Labor Union Women (CLUW)
815 Sixteenth Street NW, Washington, DC   20006
(202) 508-6969 • fax: (202) 508-6968
e-mail: csrosenblatt@cluw.org
website: www.cluw.org

Founded in 1974, the Coalition of Labor Union Women (CLUW) is America's only national organization for union women. Its primary mission is to unify all union women in a viable organization to determine the common problems and concerns of women in the workplace and to develop action programs within the framework of existing unions. CLUW's website offers information about its programs, including the Making Change at Walmart Campaign and the Contraceptive Equity Project.

Institute for Women's Policy Research (IWPR)
1200 Eighteenth Street NW, Suite 301, Washington, DC   20036
(202) 785-5100
e-mail: iwpr@iwpr.org
website: www.iwpr.org

The Institute for Women's Policy Research (IWPR) is a think tank that focuses on women's issues, including employment, economic change, and work and family. The organization conducts research and circulates its findings to address the needs of women; encourage public dialogue; and strengthen families, communities, and societies. Among other publications, IWPR publishes the *Quarterly Newsletter, Research News Roundup*, and reports such as "Occupational Segregation and the Gender Wage Gap: A Job Half Done."

National Association for Female Executives (NAFE)

2 Park Avenue, New York, NY   10016
e-mail: nafe@bonniercorp.com
website: www.nafe.com

The National Association for Female Executives (NAFE) is one of the largest associations for women professionals and women business owners in the United States. Through education, networking, and public advocacy, the organization provides resources and services to help its members achieve career success and financial security. NAFE publishes the e-newsletter *NAFE News & Notes*, which features articles such as "5 Tips for More Effective Self-Promotion" and "5 Tips on the Importance of an Open Mind for Success in Business." Its website offers feature articles, the *Nafe Café Blog*, and personal stories from its members.

National Partnership for Women & Families

1875 Connecticut Avenue NW, Suite 650
Washington, DC   20009
(202) 986-2600 • fax: (202) 986-2539
e-mail: info@nationalpartnership.org
website: www.nationalpartnership.org

The National Partnership for Women & Families is a nonprofit, nonpartisan organization that fights for major policy advancements that help women and families. As a voice on the issues that are most important to women and families, the organization advocates for family-friendly workplace policies and fights discrimination in all forms. On its website, the organization provides reports, issue briefs, and fact sheets, including "Survivors of Domestic and Sexual Violence Need Paid 'Safe Days'" and "Not Enough Family-Friendly Policies: High Stakes for Women and Families."

National Women's Law Center (NWLC)

11 Dupont Circle NW, #800, Washington, DC   20036
(202) 588-5180 • fax: (202) 588-5185
e-mail: info@nwlc.org
website: www.nwlc.org

The National Women's Law Center (NWLC) is an organization that works to expand, defend, and promote women's rights at every stage of the legal process. Women's issues the organization focuses on include employment, family security, and economic security. NWLC publishes testimony, reports, fact sheets, and issue briefs, including "Underpaid & Overloaded: Women in Low-Wage Jobs" and "Higher State Minimum Wages Promote Fair Pay for Women."

Women Employed (WE)

65 E. Wacker Place, Suite 1500, Chicago, IL   60601
(312) 782-3902 • fax: (312) 782-5249
e-mail: info@womenemployed.org
website: womenemployed.org

Women Employed (WE) is a nonprofit advocacy organization that fights to outlaw pay discrimination, pregnancy discrimination, and sexual harassment for women in the workplace. Since its inception in 1973, WE has brought together people and organizations to improve women's economic status by expanding employment opportunities. In addition to its print newsletter *WE News* and e-newsletter *WE-Zine*, WE publishes reports and fact sheets on the status of working women, including "40 and Forward: 2012/2013 Annual Report" and "Facts About Working Women."

Women Working Worldwide

521 Royal Exchange, Manchester   M2 7EN
  UK
+44 161 408 5038
e-mail: contact@women-ww.org
website: www.women-ww.org

Based in the United Kingdom, Women Working Worldwide conducts collaborative research and campaign initiatives with partners worldwide to empower women to fight for their rights as workers. Since its founding in 1985, the organization has empowered women workers in international supply chains to claim their rights, improve their working conditions, and be rewarded equitably for their work. Its publications include a newsletter and the "Report of the Campaign on Maternity Leave Made by Women Working Worldwide (WWW) and Factory Workers Union (FAWU)," which are available on its website.

Bibliography of Books

Barbara Annis and John Gray · *Work with Me: The 8 Blind Spots Between Men and Women in Business.* New York: Palgrave Macmillan, 2013.

Jessica Bacal, ed. · *Mistakes I Made at Work: 25 Influential Women Reflect on What They Got Out of Getting It Wrong.* New York: Plume, 2014.

Ellen Pinkos Cobb · *Bullying, Violence, Harassment, Discrimination, and Stress: Emerging Workplace Health and Safety Issues.* Seattle, WA: CreateSpace, 2013.

Deborah C. England · *The Essential Guide to Handling Workplace Harassment & Discrimination.* 2nd ed. Berkeley, CA: Nolo, 2012.

Catherine Fox · *7 Myths About Women and Work.* Sydney, Australia: University of New South Wales Press, 2012.

Kathleen Gerson · *The Unfinished Revolution: Coming of Age in a New Era of Gender, Work, and Family.* New York: Oxford University Press, 2011.

Victoria Gordon · *Maternity Leave: Policy and Practice.* Boca Raton, FL: CRC Press, 2013.

Heidi Gottfried · *Gender, Work, and Economy: Unpacking the Global Economy.* Malden, MA: Polity Press, 2012.

Cathy Harris	*Discrimination 101: The Complete Guide to Recognizing and Surviving Discrimination in the Workplace.* Atlanta, GA: Angels Press, 2012.
Rebekah Heppner	*The Lost Leaders: How Corporate America Loses Women Leaders.* New York: Palgrave Macmillan, 2013.
Bernie D. Jones, ed.	*Women Who Opt Out: The Debate over Working Mothers and Work-Family Balance.* New York: New York University Press, 2012.
Lilly Ledbetter with Lanier Scott Isom	*Grace and Grit: My Fight for Equal Pay and Fairness at Goodyear and Beyond.* New York: Three Rivers Press, 2013.
Maura McAdam	*Female Entrepreneurship.* New York: Routledge, 2013.
Tuuli Messer-Bookman	*Close Quarters: A Woman's Guide to Living and Working in Masculine Environments.* Atglen, PA: Schiffer Publishing, 2011.
Tara Om	*How to Successfully Overcome Sexual Harassment and Discrimination: And Get a New Job.* Seattle, WA: CreateSpace, 2014.
Janet Pucino	*Not in the Club: An Executive Woman's Journey Through the Biased World of Business.* Beverly Hills, CA: Deep Canyon Media, 2013.

Selena Rezvani	*Pushback: How Smart Women Ask—and Stand Up—for What They Want.* San Francisco, CA: Jossey-Bass, 2012.
Suzanne Riss and Teresa Palagano	*Working Mom Survival Guide: How to Run Around Less & Enjoy Life More.* San Francisco, CA: Weldon Owen, 2011.
Sarah Rutherford	*Women's Work, Men's Cultures: Overcoming Resistance and Changing Organizational Cultures.* New York: Palgrave Macmillan, 2011.
Sheryl Sandberg	*Lean In: Women, Work, and the Will to Lead.* New York: Alfred A. Knopf, 2013.
Sheryl Sandberg	*Lean In for Graduates.* New York: Alfred A. Knopf, 2014.
Debora L. Spar	*Wonder Women: Sex, Power, and the Quest for Perfection.* New York: Farrar, Straus and Giroux, 2013.
Joan C. Williams and Rachel Dempsey	*What Works for Women at Work: Four Patterns Working Women Need to Know.* New York: New York University Press, 2014.
Marcy Williams	*He vs. She: Women and the Gender Pay Gap.* Seattle, WA: CreateSpace, 2014.
Alison Wolf	*The XX Factor: How Seventy Million Working Women Created a New Society.* New York: Crown Publishers, 2013.

Index

F